DEWEY
AND EDUCATION

Dewey and Education presents Dewey's perspectives on moral psychology and development, human nature, and democratic community-building as they inform the influential philosopher's deep commitment to educational reform. In this personal yet far-reaching account, Walter Feinberg relates Dewey's work both to contemporary social and political affairs and to his own philosophical and political commitments. Written for scholars and students of the Philosophy of Education, Educational Policy Studies, and Political Theory, this book is indispensable as a guide to Dewey's influence on democratic education.

Walter Feinberg is the Charles Dunn Hardie Professor Emeritus of Educational Policy Studies at the University of Illinois. He received a Lifetime Achievement Award from the John Dewey Society in 2014.

Routledge Key Ideas in Education Series

Series Editors: Bob Lingard and Fazal Rizvi
Founding Editors: Greg Dimitriadis and Bob Lingard

Freud and Education, Deborah P. Britzman
Marx and Education, Jean Anyon
Foucault, Power, and Education, Stephen J. Ball
L.S. Vygotsky and Education, Luis C. Moll
Freire and Education, Antonia Darder
Literacy and Education, James Gee
Du Bois and Education, Carl A. Grant
Dewey and Education, Walter Feinberg

DEWEY
AND EDUCATION

WALTER FEINBERG

NEW YORK AND LONDON

First published 2018
by Routledge
711 Third Avenue, New York, NY 10017

and by Routledge
2 Park Square, Milton Park, Abingdon, Oxon, OX14 4RN

Routledge is an imprint of the Taylor & Francis Group, an informa business

© 2018 Taylor & Francis

The right of Walter Feinberg to be identified as author of this work has been asserted by him in accordance with sections 77 and 78 of the Copyright, Designs and Patents Act 1988.

All rights reserved. No part of this book may be reprinted or utilised in any form or by any electronic, mechanical, or other means, now known or hereafter invented, including photocopying and recording, or in any information storage or retrieval system, without permission in writing from the publishers.

Trademark notice: Product or corporate names may be trademarks or registered trademarks, and are used only for identification and explanation without intent to infringe.

Library of Congress Cataloging-in-Publication Data
A catalog record for this title has been requested

ISBN: 978-1-138-65771-7 (hbk)
ISBN: 978-1-138-65770-0 (pbk)
ISBN: 978-1-351-04979-5 (ebk)

Typeset in Minion
by Apex CoVantage, LLC

For my wife, Eleanor, my eternal inspiration and love.

CONTENTS

SERIES EDITORS' INTRODUCTION	viii
PREFACE	ix
ACKNOWLEDGMENTS	xxv
1 Introduction	1
2 Influences on Dewey and the Development of Pragmatism	14
3 Dewey's Philosophy	38
4 Dewey on Education	71
5 Toward a New Progressive Educational Movement	103
INDEX	127

SERIES EDITORS' INTRODUCTION

This series introduces key people and topics and discusses their particular implications for the field of education. Written by the most prominent thinkers in the field, these "key ideas" are read through the series' authors' past and present work, with particular attention given to the ways these ideas can, do, and might impact theory, research, practice and policy in education.

More specifically, these texts offer particular conversations with prominent authors whose work has resonated across education and related fields. Books in this series read as conversations with authorities whose thinking has helped constitute these ideas and their role in the field of education—yesterday, today and tomorrow.

Much more than introductions alone, these short, virtuosic volumes look to shape ongoing discussions in the field of education by putting the field's contemporary luminaries in dialogue with its foundational figures and critical topics. From new students to senior scholars, these volumes will spark the imaginations of a range of readers thinking through key ideas and education.

PREFACE

Introduction

The invitation to write a book on John Dewey (1859–1952), and his influence on my own work, provides a rare opportunity to reflect on one of the major sources of my ideas and to extend them in a new direction. I have studied and written about Dewey on and off since I was a graduate student. I have analyzed his ideas; I have defended and have criticized them, but I had never really thought about why I have been attracted to his writings in the first place or how he has influenced my own thoughts. The invitation provided an opportunity to reflect on that influence and its impact on my work as an educational philosopher.

This book will mark the third time that I have undertaken a major project on Dewey. The first was my dissertation, *A Comparative Study of the Social Philosophies of John Dewey and Bernard Bosanquet* (1966).[1] The dissertation, written for a philosophical audience, was concerned with the question of social pluralism and political legitimacy. The second time was in my first book, *Reason and Rhetoric, the Intellectual*

Foundations of Twentieth Century Liberal Educational Reform (1974).[2] The audience for that book was educators and educational policy makers. Although both offered criticisms of Dewey, the tone was different: The first was a friendly criticism; the second much less so. The first criticized his value theory; the second his politics and his educational work. The second was much sharper and more controversial than the first. In the dissertation, I argue that Dewey confounded value claims with factual ones and in short committed what philosophers call "the naturalistic fallacy." In the book, I questioned whether Dewey's liberalism was adequate to address the legitimate restraints on government power and the appropriate division between intelligence—as exercised by disinterested scholars—and power as exercised by government. I also questioned whether Dewey went deep enough in his criticism of capitalism, suggesting that he did not adequately challenge the industrial division of labor that maintained it. I highlighted aspects of his educational writings that seemed to implicitly accede to the existing class structure, even granted that he was critical of its harshest effects. Some of my criticisms went against the grain of Dewey scholarship at the time, but I still believe that most can hold up to scrutiny. What has changed, however, is the educational and political context in which these claims were made, and this calls for a new assessment of Dewey's impact on American thought and education.

Although Dewey himself could be sharply critical of many features of American society he is rightly seen as a philosopher of progress and as a quintessential American philosopher.[3] Since the idea of progress has come under significant criticism at least since the 1970s, it will be useful to explain just how this designation fits Dewey.

Was Dewey a Progressive Educator?

Educational theorists often identify Dewey as the founder of progressive education, which they identify with child-centered instruction. This is partly accurate, but only partly. There were many people who contributed to the idea of child-centered education, and Dewey was only one of them. Dewey himself called Francis Parker (1837–1902) "the Father of Progressive Education." Also, it may be that the Head Teacher at his University of Chicago Laboratory School, Ella Flagg Young (1845–1918) (Dewey called her the "wisest person in school matters with whom he had come in contact in any way"),[4] made more important contributions to progressive pedagogy than did Dewey.

Dewey is most important for education because he understood that democracy requires a certain kind of person, and he believed that the development of this kind of person would be the primary responsibility of public schools. Dewey is a child-centered educator, not because of any romantic view of childhood, but because he understood that the basic values of democracy needed to be socially constructed. In other words, without using the phrase, he developed the idea of a democratic intersubjective character—or a collective understanding that the basic values of equality, freedom, inquiry and mutual growth are ideals that citizens should be able to internalize and to assume are present in others.

Dewey believed that democratic character development was the critical task of the schools. Child centered education was critical to him because the active engagement of children is essential if they are to grow into democratic citizens. Democracy requires that obedience to arbitrary traditional authority be replaced by the authority based on open inquiry and the scientific method. The democratic teacher does not promote learning by withholding rewards or by threat of punishment. Rather, the democratic teacher sets the stage for cooperative learning by engaging the student in meaningful activities.

Dewey did not believe, as did some romantics, that a child's wishes should always be indulged. For Dewey, teachers were still the authority; they set the stage for learning through meaningful active engagement. The teacher's special task was to both honor and enlist the logic of the child as a pathway to helping the child grasp the logic of the subject matter. The world was changing, and this meant that a new, more open kind of citizen would be needed as well. His progressive educational philosophy and his liberal political ideas were designed to develop this kind of citizen.

The Meanings of Liberalism

A brief word is perhaps in order about what I mean by liberalism. At the time I wrote my first book, *Reason and Rhetoric*, the term "neo-liberalism," if it had been invented, was not very much in vogue. Indeed, the term "neo-liberalism" today covers much of what Dewey and his followers derisively called "classical-liberalism" or "old individualism," which they criticized for promoting excessive competition, greed and unregulated market capitalism while justifying labor exploitation. The confusion is that Dewey called his alternative "new liberalism."

Dewey's "new liberalism" in many ways stands opposed to what today goes under the label "neo-liberalism." Dewey's new liberalism includes a heavy dose of market regulation, scientific social planning, labor input, cooperative relations, and considerable government regulation. Neo-liberalism greatly resembles what Dewey termed the old, or classical, liberalism. The new liberals believed "that the system of industry for profit without regard to social consequences had in fact a most unfavorable effect upon the real liberty of the mass of individuals."[5] However, Dewey did not accept the Marxist view that violent revolution was the best way to achieve meaningful change, and his ideas on education can be read in part as a response to Marx's idea that the proletariat through violent revolution would serve as the agent of effective advancement. For Dewey, the teacher was a much more promising agent for social progress.

Dewey associated his new liberalism with many historical progressive social changes from the abolition of slavery, to prison reform, to woman suffrage. And at a time that dictators were coming into power in Europe, Dewey argued that the new liberalism must be as much concerned with the *means* for achieving large, desirable social goals, as it is with the character of the goals themselves. Large social change was permissible, often imperative, but only if it were accomplished through humane, experimental, democratic procedures. Undesirable means cancels out desirable ends.

One of Dewey's concerns was the extreme fluctuation of market capitalism a fluctuation culminated in the suffering brought on by the Great Depression. His political philosophy promoted cooperative, scientific planning that would minimize fluctuation and promote the public good. Although there were many to the left of Dewey who argued for more sweeping change, he was still perceived as a radical to many who held that government intervention was socialism that would distort the basic laws of the market and trample on the rights of the individual.

Today, Dewey might point to the Scandinavian countries and Western Europe as examples of what he had in mind. To some degree, Dewey's ideas were more similar to those of the economist John M. Keynes who promoted government intervention in markets than Milton Friedman who opposed it. But as Friedman once said, "We are all Keynesians now," a remark that is often wrongly attributed to Richard Nixon. Dewey would add that liberalism should also be concerned with the development of social interdependence for the sake of human flourishing. Flourishing requires both bottom-up as well as top-down planning guided by scientific inquiry.

Dewey and Me

The editor of this series has asked me to address the influence that Dewey has had on my own work but here I want to address a prior question: Why did I become interested in Dewey and in philosophy in the first place? My interest first developed when I was a graduate student at Boston University (BU) in the early 1960s, just as Dewey's star was fading from the philosophical universe.

Even though many philosophy departments were concentrating on linguistic philosophy at the time, BU was not. Its focus was the history of philosophy, and Dewey had arguably been among the most influential American philosophers and one of its most influential public intellectual in the first half of the twentieth century. Hence, while no seminar in Dewey was taught in the Philosophy Department, as opposed to seminars on Kant, Hegel, Whitehead, Quine etc., he was a significant presence in the courses, and he was recognized for his influence on twentieth-century ideas.

Historically, the Philosophy Department at BU had been at the forefront of a philosophical school of thought labeled Boston Personalism. Personalism grew out of the Methodist Church and had a significant influence on the Church's development in the early part of the twentieth century. As a commuter student, I had little awareness of this history. BU was but a streetcar ride away from my home, and at the time I entered the graduate program, the Department was becoming intellectually more diverse. It added a philosopher of science, a philosopher of aesthetics, a phenomenologist and a Dewey scholar alongside of philosophers of religion. Indeed, one of its claims to fame was its eclecticism. The Methodist influence, although present, was hardly noticeable to me when I was a graduate student.

BU had a system of doctoral advising where two faculty members, called Readers, supervised a student's dissertation research. Dewey had had an influence on both of my readers. Marx Wartofsky (1928–1997), my first reader, finished his graduate work at Columbia after Dewey's death but while his influence was still strong. He worked in aesthetics and philosophy of science. I gravitated to him because of his interest in political philosophy, especially the work of Hegel and Marx, and in contemporary critical theorists. Kenneth Benne (1908–1992), my second reader, had served as Dewey's assistant during the late 1930s and was a major figure in the reconstruction of Dewey's educational ideas. He was also a leader in an application of group dynamic theory (called T groups), which encouraged collective reflection on behavior in groups.

Although Boston Personalism and Dewey's Pragmatism differed a great deal, they shared the view that philosophy should be useful in helping to make a more humane world. BU's most famous alumnus, Martin Luther King (1929–1968), would come to epitomize that view for the entire nation, but it was also present in smaller ways. For example, Harold C. Case, the Methodist Minister and President of BU at that time, hired Wartofsky, who had been blacklisted from many universities during the McCarthy era. Wartofsky recounted to me that when he was interviewed for his position at BU, Case asked him to tell him in detail about the activities that led to his blacklisting. When Wartofsky finished telling the President about the black listing, Case thanked him and said that now if anyone asked whether he knew of Wartofsky's background, he could honestly say that he did.

A similar situation may have occurred when Benne was hired as the Berenson Professor of Human Relations by Case. Benne told me that at the time of his arrival at BU he was quite sick, and Case put him up at the President's house as he recovered. I suspect that Case also knew—since it was in the local Champaign paper—that Benne had been forced to resign from the University of Illinois, where he had been outed as a homosexual.

At the time I entered the graduate college, I did not know any of this, nor did I know that my own education would ironically owe a heavy debt to both McCarthyism and to homophobia and to the welcoming protection of progressive intellectuals by the Methodist minister who served as president of BU during the time I was a student there. In any event, it was clear that I was drawn to philosophy in part because I believed that ideas mattered in practice, and so did a number of the BU professors.

The Fading of Dewey's Influence

Dewey galvanized social thought and political engagement in support of the ideas of progressive liberal democracy, but by the time I began to read his works, other philosophical ideas were influencing mainstream American philosophical thought. The foremost ones, broadly labeled linguistic philosophy, came from Great Britain and focused on the function and use of language. Sandra Laugier identifies two tasks of this import. The first was to create an ideal or formal language that would clarify everyday use. The second was to "examine the multiplicity of uses of common languages."[6] Part of the first task involved exposing ideological excesses and was not inconsistent with much of Dewey's task to advance systematic inquiry. The second narrowed the scope of philosophy to an inquiry about language, a constriction that Dewey objected to.

These philosophers wanted to bring philosophy out of what they saw as the dark ages and make it a handmaiden to science. No doubt, many of them also hoped that a better understanding of language might serve to blunt the emotional appeals of fascism, communism and other ideological movements. To the extent that obscure language and pseudo-science helped to spark the rise of anti-democratic thought and totalitarianism, these philosophers were on the same side as was Dewey, although their understanding of the task of philosophy differed.

In addition to linguistic philosophy, another import, Existentialism, arrived from the European Continent. It was a response to the devastation and inhumanity of the Second World War. Like Boston Personalism, it was concerned with the problem of evil, but existentialists were *not* trying to explain how a benevolent God could allow evil to exist—the question for personalism. The question for post-WWII Existentialism was how it is possible to live after the Holocaust—a life without God and without reason. As the Existential Philosopher Jean Paul Sartre (1905–1980) wrote: "If God had gone into retreat during the Holocaust, then reason had also gone into hiding and philosophy had been rendered irrelevant." Or, as the philosopher Theodore Adorno (1903–1969) famously wrote: "*To write poetry after Auschwitz is barbaric.*"

Although Dewey had a well-developed theory of human development, he did not have a well-developed theory of evil, and his optimistic view of progress seemed to many out of keeping with the times. Unlike Dewey's pragmatism, existentialism recognized evil as more than just clash of goods. Evil was a lived reality. Unlike personalism, it addressed the *surd*, or unexplainable human suffering, without sugarcoating it in terms of God, and without the assumptions of a divine plan or of an existence with any pre-established meaning stamped onto it. And it rejected the basic assumption of the Enlightenment that human knowledge was limitless, an assumption that Dewey never fully questioned.

There had been elements of existential thought in other philosophers such as Hegel (1770–1831), especially in his powerful "Master Slave"[7] narrative. As in Existentialism, Hegel saw freedom as the essential characteristic of human beings, but it was not a given. It was rather an achievement. Hegel held that the self is a process of development toward self-consciousness and that it is developed in the context of and through other selves. Full freedom involves the recognition of the role of the other in the formation of the self. Hegel provided an opening for both Marx (1818–1883) and Dewey and served as a powerful counter to the story told by classical liberal thinkers such as John Locke (1862–1704), whose political philosophy presupposed already formed individuals, with fully developed wills.

As mentioned earlier the reason education was so important for Dewey was because he believed that character formation was critical for democracy and that schools held out the greatest possibility for developing interdependent democratic individuals connected through mutual recognition of that interdependence. Dewey did not use the contemporary term "intersubjectivity" to describe this mutual recognition, but it would fit here. It suggests the mutual outlook and values that one person holds and can assume all other people hold as well.

Dewey and Bosanquet

I became seriously interested in Dewey through the work of his disciple and one of my teachers, the educational philosopher Kenneth Benne, who, in addition to his appointments in Education and Philosophy, held the Chair in Human Relations at BU. Benne combined Dewey's pragmatism with the social theory of Kurt Lewin (1890–1947) and used the resulting hybrid to study conflict resolution in small groups, called T groups. He was a good applied philosopher, and when I became his assistant, I began to see a practical side to philosophy.

Before I met Benne, I had written a master's thesis under Wartofsky's supervision on Hegel's concept of property,[8] and I still had Hegel on my mind as I began to consider a topic for my dissertation. I chose to do a comparative study on Dewey's and Bernard Bosanquet's (1848–1923) social philosophy. Bosanquet was a British Hegelian and social reformer who, like Hegel, presented a moral argument for the authority of the state.[9] The dissertation examined the different conceptions of pluralism in their social philosophies. It also offered a number of criticisms of Dewey and suggested that Bosanquet had a view of the state that provided a useful supplement.

Still influenced by Hegel, the dissertation provided a rather abstract and inadequate definition of pluralism as "the form of Society in which differences are both maintained and unified."[10] Had I written the dissertation in a later period, I would have provided different examples of the kind of groups that could be identified as pluralistically different—class, racial, religious, gender/LGBT groups. Still, at its most basic level, pluralism entails the issue of state legitimacy, e.g. how much legitimate control can a state place on the various groups that comprise it, and what are the appropriate limits of state authority? Since I wrote the dissertation, I have extended the inquiry by addressing issues of group identity and culture.[11] The question of legitimate state authority over the education of its citizens continues to be one of my significant interests.

Summary of Dissertation

From the point of view of more than fifty years of hindsight, it is not too difficult to see that the dissertation was partial and incomplete, but it did set the stage for a good deal of my later work which challenged the adequacy of Dewey's social theory. I argued that Bosanquet's view of the state complemented Dewey's pluralism. I argued too that Bosanquet could be interpreted as setting as a condition for loyalty to the state the extent to which a state facilitates individual flourishing. True, there is another way to read Bosanquet as justifying British colonialism by idealizing the state and not challenging the rigid class system. For example, his contemporary and fellow Hegelian Bradley (1846–1924) had written an essay titled "My Station and Its Duties," which promoted a static hierarchy of duties and obligations and which was not necessarily inconsistent with Bosanquet's ideas.

Bradley's ideal, today portrayed in its decline in British TV imports such as *Upstairs/Downstairs* and *Downton Abbey*, was the reigning idea of British imperialism. Ishiguro's tragic/comic novel *Remains of the Day* shows this ideal in all its folly in the wake of post-war anti-colonialism. Yet I felt that the idea could be removed from its nineteenth-century colonialist context and expressed in terms of the continuing need for social cohesion where different people understand their own limits and appreciate the way in which the activity of others supplement and enrich their own existence.[12] This was not that different from the very justification that Dewey himself offered for education where each individual learns to identify, develop and expand their own interests within the community as a whole.[13]

For Hegelians, this whole was labeled the "Absolute," which, to the modern ear, sounds totalizing, if not just weird, but which for Bradley, Bosanquet and other Hegelians provided a context where one's life took on a meaning in service to others. What it suggested to Bosanquet was an ideal of connectedness and completeness.

In the final analysis, Bosanquet's political state looms too large for my taste, and for Dewey as well. Yet Bosanquet may be read generously as suggesting a standard for human well-being that the good state must provide, a standard for satisfying individual wills. As an example, he writes:

> How can Smith will to go to town by train without willing the existence of the railway . . . the object of other wills than his own, which must be true if it is to be possible for him to go to town by train.[14]

I concluded the dissertation by combining the insight of Dewey about participation with my interpretation of Bosanquet about the requirements for a good state, arguing that the inclusiveness of the state, as a measure of its goodness, must involve not only a sharing of its benefits but also participation in the creation of its goals. This was an implicit definition for democratic pluralism—social cohesion in the context of significant differences. However, for Dewey, the aim would not be cohesion and completeness as it was for Bosanquet, but cohesion and openness, where participation in shaping future development would be a part of political and cultural formation. Still the balance between plurality and the cohesion, between cultural difference and national unity, remained to be addressed and served to frame my larger research program.

A Preview of the Book

I agree with Louis Menand[15] that pragmatism arose partly as a response to the massive destruction brought about by the Civil War, and I propose in this book that Dewey's educational philosophy grew out of this project. Its aim was to develop *a new* American identity, one that cut across traditional geographical boundaries—north, south, old world, new—and that was based on scientific inquiry and democratic ideals. I also argue that this project was conducted under a pervasive social imaginary—the way people think about themselves collectively—of progress, optimism and trust, and that this social imaginary continued well into the twentieth century. The major task of Dewey's educational and political philosophy was to promote this identity through schools and other institutions. To look closely at Dewey and his ideas, as I do in the chapters that follow, is to attempt to understand the possibilities and the limitations of this imaginary of progress.

I conclude the book by noting the limits of this imaginary for postmodern times and argue that it is time for a new form of progressive education, one that would recognize structural and systematic inequality and that would promote a more equitable distribution of resources and power. This new progressive education would have a critical dimension. Students would understand the ways in which benefits are developed and distributed in American society. It would have a creative dimension. Students would develop the ethical and aesthetic capacity to imagine alternative realities. And, it would have an academic dimension. Students would develop the scientific, communicative, interpretive and *political* skills that promote effective agency and meaning.

After examining the influence of Charles S. Peirce and William James on Dewey's philosophy and on the social imaginary of their times in Chapter 2, in Chapters 3 and 4 I take a closer look at different aspects of Dewey's philosophy, showing how Dewey's conception of meaning bridges his ideas on education and his ideas on democracy and education. I conclude by showing the limitations of the social imaginary that guided Dewey and some of the overlooked resources in Dewey's philosophy that can be used to address these limitations.

Notes

1. Walter Feinberg, *A Comparative Study of the Social Philosophies of John Dewey and Bernard Bosanquet* (Boston: Boston University, unpublished dissertation, 1966).
2. Walter Feinberg, *Reason and Rhetoric, the Intellectual Foundations of Twentieth Century Liberal Educational Reform* (New York: John Wiley, 1974).
3. Morton White, *Social Thought in America: The Revolt against Formalism* (Boston: Beacon Press, 1957).
4. L. Dean Webb and Martha McCarthy, "Ella Flagg Young: Pioneer of Democracy," *Educational Administration Quarterly* (April 1, 1998), http://journals.sagepub.com/doi/abs/10.1177/0013161X98034002004
5. Ibid., p. 201.
6. Sandra Laugier, *Why We Need Ordinary Language Philosophy*, trans. Daniella Ginsburg (Chicago: University of Chicago Press, 2013), p. 10.
7. Georg W. F. Hegel, *The Phenomenology of Mind*, trans. J. B. Baillie (London: George Allen & Unwin, 1910/1951), pp. 228–240.

8. Walter Feinberg, *The Place of Property in Hegel's Concept of the State* (Boston: Boston University, unpublished Master's thesis, 1962).
9. See Peter Gordon and John White, *Philosophers as Educational Reformers: The Influence of Idealism on British Educational Thought and Practice* (London: Routledge and Kegan Paul, 1979).
10. Ibid., Abstract, p. 1.
11. Walter Feinberg, *Common Schools/Uncommon Identities: National Unity and Cultural Difference* (New Haven: Yale University Press, 1998).
12. Ibid., p. 285.
13. John Dewey, *Democracy and Education* (New York: The Free Press, 1916).
14. Bernard Bosanquet, "The Notion of the General Will," *Mind*, 29 (1920), p. 78.
15. Louis Menand, *The Metaphysical Club: The Story of Ideas in America* (New York: Farrar, Straus and Giroux, 2001).

ACKNOWLEDGMENTS

I am especially indebted to my friend and colleague Eric Bredo for his very careful reading of this manuscript and for his many corrections and suggestions. I owe a long unacknowledged debt to my late teachers at Boston University who introduced me to philosophy. They include Peter Bertocci, John Lavely and Richard Millard, who helped me to see why the problems of philosophy mattered. And, I owe a special debt to the late Marx Wartofsty, for his insistence on rigor, and to the late Ken Benne, for his kindness and humanity and for his creative appropriation of Dewey.

And, as always, to my loving wife Eleanor, for her years of support and for our loving children and grandchildren.

1

INTRODUCTION

Dewey: A Quintessential American Philosopher

John Dewey represents a third leg to the evasive idea of a democratic education. The first leg *is usually represented* by Thomas Jefferson (1743–1826) and his idea of a meritocratic rather than an aristocratic basis for education and leadership. In other words, leaders were to be chosen and educated because of their ability rather than because of their birthright. Of course, Jefferson famously compromised his own ideal by the 700 slaves he owned throughout his life, none of whom ever had any chance of developing their innate talent of potential. The second leg *is usually represented by* Horace Mann's (1796–1859) idea of universal, compulsory education, an ideal that took decades to realize in even a rudimentary way. Dewey *can be said to represent* a third leg. He held that a democratic society requires a *democratic* education. This too remains an aspirational ideal, but one whose meaning is certainly worth aspiring to and developing.

First, a caveat: To say that the Jefferson, Mann and Dewey could be said to represent three legs of the democratic ideal should not be read as a heroic view of American history or of their ideas. Such a view undercuts the struggles of everyday people, workers, women, black people and Native Americans, gays and others to build a more inclusive democracy. This is why, as I have suggested elsewhere, philosophy of education is first and foremost a street philosophy.[1] It begins, as Dewey would note, with the felt needs and common concerns that develop out of the everyday experiences of people. I use the metaphor of "three legs" to suggest that democracy has both stable and unstable elements and that the development of an education that is consistent with democracy is always an unfinished task. And, it is also suggested that the idea of democracy itself is incomplete, requiring constant refreshment and renewal. Three legs are enough to support a structure, but they are also unstable. The structure can collapse, or new supports need to be developed. In this book, I show how Dewey represents a third leg to the basic ideas of democracy and also why that support is incomplete. In the last chapter, I suggest some of the avenues for constructing new supports.

Another caveat: None of the above should be taken as an endorsement of the claim that democracy has ever fully flourished in America. Nor, however, should it be taken to endorse the more cynical view that the idea of democracy is simply a cover for the powerful to exploit the powerless. In my view, democracy as practiced in United States is certainly flawed. It is distorted by the influence of wealth over the electoral system, the courts and education. It is distorted by the unequal influence of corporate wealth on educational policy and on the content of the curriculum. Nevertheless, the ability to recognize and address these flaws is critical for democratic reconstruction and for democratic education.

Focus on the Idea, Not Just Its Agent

The *idea* of progress toward democracy is a two-edge sword. On the one edge, it allows some of the founding ideas of American democracy to be clarified, sharpened, modified and redefined. On the other edge, it exposes those who represent these ideas to the charge of hypocrisy because they lived between two conflicting worlds—the actual everyday world governed by the old idea—in Jefferson's case, the world where slavery was an everyday fact—and the idea of a yet-to-be-realized world—again, for Jefferson, a world where *all* are equal. To realize the ideal requires telling the truth, in so far as we can understand it, about the past. This task should be a major task of democratic education, wherever it is carried out, in schools, or through monuments or in museums.

For Dewey, education is not just *preparation* for democracy (or anything else), although certainly, that is a desirable outcome. Rather, education must be democratic if it is to be truly education. Anything else is at best mere schooling and, at worst, miseducative. What Dewey meant by the idea that democracy requires a democratic education is the topic of this book. However, he did not mean that students should vote on what they should learn or on how they should learn it. Nor did he mean that teachers should simply abandon their authority and let each child determine their own course of study. Rather, a democratic education was about meaning and human flourishing in the context of community.

We are used to thinking of democracy in political terms, but for Dewey, political democracy was but one rather narrow aspect of democratic education. One of his most important insights is that political democracy is a very limited form of democracy and that voting is but a small part of the true democratic spirit. A culture of democracy is every bit as important as a politics of democracy, and indeed, political democracy depends on cultural democracy. A culture that fosters democratic values is one that promotes openness to possibilities and that encourages systematic inquiry to resolve differences.

Dewey and the Post-Civil War Project

Pragmatism, the philosophical movement with which Dewey is identified, arose out of the aftermath of the destruction and antagonism of the American Civil War. It was a forward-looking movement whose temperament embodied openness, freedom, science, experimentation and future possibilities while rejecting certainty, dogmatism and determinism.[2] The task that Lincoln bequeathed "to bind up the Nation's wounds" became an unspoken task for Pragmatism.

The progressive education movement, with which Dewey was identified, was also a part of this post-Civil War temperament. Its task was to educate children to embrace science, to respect evidence, to solve problems peacefully and to be open to new possibilities in a new and ever more interdependent world. The movement was called *progressive* education for a reason. Its followers believed that this new world, a world of electric lights, of motorcars and airplanes, of mass production and cheap goods, brought huge challenges and equally huge possibilities. The task of philosophy was to develop the intellectual tools that would enable these challenges to be addressed and new possibilities to emerge. The task of education was to produce a modern generation equipped with a new form of consciousness able to take advantage of the innovations that science and technology was developing. For Dewey, public schools provided the single most promising vehicle for addressing these changes and public school teachers were, as he put it, "the prophet of the true God."[3] Teachers were to be the new interpreters of the past and the era's most inspired and effective change agent. Dewey believed that progressive, peaceful, scientifically guided social change was possible and that a progressive educational system, with a knowledgeable and committed teaching force, could make it probable. It is hard to tell on what this belief was based—faith, hope or science, but Dewey was not alone in holding it.

The Idea of a Social Imaginary

Dewey's vision drew from and contributed to the collective, or intersubjective, way in which many—although certainly not all—Americans, made sense of their everyday lives during the earlier part of the twentieth century. The philosopher Charles Taylor calls this intersubjective understanding a social imaginary.[4] A social imaginary involves the way people imagine their social existence, the way different roles fit together with one another, the expectations that people expect to be normally met and "the deeper normative notions and images which underlie these expectations." It is the understanding that you and I share, that we know we share and that as such makes communication and coordinated action possible.

To see what Taylor is getting at by his idea of a social imaginary consider as a point of contrast a description by the Japanese psychiatrist, Takeo Doi, of his reaction on his first visit to America. After a supervisor did him some favor, Doi responded not with a "thank you," but with "I am sorry," which, of course, compelled his supervisor to ask, "what are you sorry about?" Doi explains to his American reader that "my difficulty in saying 'thank you' arose . . . from a feeling that it implied too great an equality with someone who was in fact my supervisor."[5] As Doi explains, his reluctance has to do with the very assumption of equality itself and with the uncomfortable idea of independence that it implies. For the Japanese, he tells the reader, the assumption of a natural equality is strange, and the assertion of independence is awkward and embarrassing. The more accepted assumption is one of hierarchy, and the more comfortable relationships are ones of interdependence. (I am told that the Japanese language has no equivalent of looking someone in the eye, since it implies an equality that is not assumed to exist.) As Doi continues in an unusually critical way:

> It is highly doubtful that all people are created equal. And even if they are, it still remains to be asked just how they are equal. Rather it is fair to suggest that Americans promote equality precisely because of what is in fact an extremely naïve belief in universal equality as self-evident truth.[6]

The point that I want to make is that each social imaginary, the Japanese and the American, as *broad stroke* examples, sets a grid or a horizon for understanding common practices and ways of thinking. It is not impossible for an American to explain the assumption of equality or independence—toned positively—to a Japanese person, but it would take a considerable amount of work to do so and even more to show how the assumption is reflected in certain American practices.

My example paints with a broad stroke and is meant to show in cultural terms how a social imaginary sets the terms of intelligibility. However, there is a temporal as well as a cultural dimension to a social imaginary that makes events in different historical periods intelligible. Consider how difference explanations, say, for example, "she is irresponsible" v. "she has an *attention deficit disorder*" for failing to turn in a homework assignment depends on whether the behavior is placed in a moral or in a clinical framework, and consider too the different implications that each has for treating the behavior.

By social imaginary, I indicate elements of our world-view that can be called upon to understand the normal expectations we have of one another[7] and what we take as reasonable to expect from each other. For Taylor, it involves a sense "of moral order," of where things are going and of where they ought to go. If this imaginary changes, then the way we evaluate a particular practice or narrative will also change. In the last chapter of this book, I show how a changing social imaginary influenced the way I have understood Dewey, and how, in the light of such change, his educational philosophy may be reimagined to construct a new leg for democratic education to rest on.

A caveat is in order here. In the last chapter, I label Dewey's social imaginary as one of trust and optimism and suggest that this became the dominant imaginary of his time. I am not suggesting, however, that there is only one social imaginary at any given time. I do believe, however, that there is often one dominant social imaginary that controls much of social discourse at any one time—some on the left would describe this as hegemonic to indicate the service that it performs for the more powerful or influential members of society. However, competing social imaginaries can exist at the same time. As I will explain in Chapter 5, this is what happened in part to the social imaginary of trust and optimism associated with Dewey's America.

The Twentieth-Century Social Imaginary

To understand the rise and fall of Dewey and American Pragmatism requires an understanding of how well they fit the social imaginary of their times. Pragmatism captured the social imaginary of twentieth-century liberal America. It was hopeful, scientific and progressive. Certainly there were dark spots—racism, economic inequality, labor discontent, economic exploitation—but these simply were problems that the social imaginary affirmed were fixable with more science, better social engineering and more economic growth.

Pragmatism declined as a sustainable movement in the middle of the century along with the progressive social imaginary that had quickened its development. The Holocaust, the Gulag, the church bombings and then the Vietnam War were reminders of the tenacity of evil and served too as reminders of the possible complicity of science in evil causes. At the same time, progressive education also lost some of its appeal. Conservatives criticized it for promoting what they called "value relativism" and an anything-goes education, while critics from the left argued that it simply served the children of the middle class and legitimized an education system that reproduced an unequal class structure.

Dewey's Legacy in Education

After his death in 1952, Dewey's influence on American philosophy declined as philosophers looked to England and continental Europe for new inspiration. Progressive education suffered a similar fate. As its ideas came under criticism, it was subject to the hysteria generated during the McCarthy era, with some very influential figures blaming it for America's purportedly weakened position in the Cold War. Critics in the 1950s and 60s wrongly claimed that progressive education was somehow inconsistent with rigorous training in math, science, engineering and foreign language, subjects thought essential for winning the Cold War. (Similar questionable claims have been repeated in recent decades as critics assail education for a purported decline in America's economic competitiveness.) Many of these claims rest on a caricature of progressive education as well as the gloomiest picture of political and economic progress, but they have fueled much recent educational reform. This reform promotes greater standardization of the schools, more rigid discipline, more high-stakes tests and reduction in teacher autonomy. Arguably, they have had the effect of discouraging some highly talented, creative and committed people from entering the teaching profession.

Still, until the 1970s, Dewey's standing among educational theorists remained largely favorable, and his influence was claimed for some of the most innovative programs such as the new math and the values clarification movements of the 1960s, the open education movement of the 1970s. Today, the feminist and critical pedagogy movements, although less likely to explicitly appeal to Dewey, still draw inspiration from his idea of a democratic community. In addition, many of his ideas, acknowledged or not, form part of the backbone of the loyal opposition in education, serving as reminders that educators must attend to more than economic and political demands. Moreover, many of the educational innovations that Dewey championed never did go away but were incorporated into the routine of schools.[8] Interestingly, Dewey's view of active learning is now incorporated into some of the bastions of traditionalism, such as medical education. One of the leaders in this movement is Dewey's own alma mater, the University of Vermont. As William Jeffries, one of its Deans, reports on Public Broadcasting:

> There is a lot of evidence that lectures are not the best way to accumulate the skills needed to become a scientist or a physician. We've seen much evidence in the literature, accumulated in the last decade, that shows that when you do a comparison between lectures and other methods of learning—typically called "active learning" methods—that lectures are not as efficient or not as successful in allowing students to accumulate knowledge in the same amount of time.[9]

That Jeffries did not invoke Dewey, the University of Vermont's most famous alumnus, is ironical evidence that progressive education has been *quietly* imbedded in the educational DNA, at least of some programs. Dewey's influence can also be seen in the nationally acclaimed work of Debbie Meier's vision for Central Park East High School in New York and Vivian Paley's efforts to build community among her kindergarten students at the University of Chicago Lab School.

Educational philosophy has been critical in sustaining Dewey's legacy through the work of Dewey scholars like Kenneth Benne, Eric Bredo, James Garrison and Leonard Waks and also through key organizations such as the John Dewey Society and its journal *Education and Culture*. Other journals, such as *Educational Theory*, frequently publish essays on Dewey. The feminist educational philosopher Nel Knoddings perhaps captures Dewey's educational influence when she writes: "Everything we do . . . as teachers has moral overtones."[10] And recently, Denis Phillips published the single most comprehensive summary of Dewey's classic *Democracy and Education*.[11]

The Continuing Influence of Dewey on Philosophy

After three decades in the philosophical wilderness, with the publication of Richard Rorty's *Philosophy and the Mirror of Nature*[12] in 1979, and the work of Hilary Putnam's *Pragmatism*[13] in 1995, Dewey scholarship experienced a significant revival in philosophy. The fact that Rorty made his early reputation as an analytic philosopher and that Putnam was a world-renown logician did not hurt. The Dewey Center at Southern Illinois University in Carbondale[14] maintains the Dewey legacy, supporting high-quality Dewey scholarship and publishing his complete works. Similar centers devoted to Dewey's work can also be found in other parts of the world, and every year, conferences are held on pragmatism and Dewey in a number of different countries. The title of *The European Journal of Pragmatism and American Philosophy* is an indication that Dewey's ideas are still alive throughout the world.

Why Dewey?

Since Dewey's death, American society and its schools have undergone a great transformation. When Dewey died in 1952, there was virtually no federal legislation regarding education, and very few court decisions affected the schools. Granted, *Pierce v. Society of the Sisters* (1925)[15] upheld the right of parents to send their children to private and religious, instead of public, schools, and *West Virginia State Board of Education v. Barnette* (1943)[16] upheld the right of religious children to refuse to salute the flag in school, but mostly all decisions concerning schools were made by state and local authorities. Even laws governing compulsory education had been a state affair. Obviously, this is no longer the case. The business of the school is now everyone's business, and most everyone has an idea about the proper responsibility of the schools, about what it should mean to educate children and even about whether the whole idea of a public education is still a viable one. Many of these views are in tension with each other, and educators and policy makers are under considerable pressure to satisfy conflicting demands.

Dewey provides an opportunity to step back from these pressures and to think about the more basic question: What is the role of education in a democratic society?[17] As Dewey so nicely put it:

> What avail is it to win prescribed amounts of information about geography and history, to win ability to read and write, if in the process the individual loses his own soul: loses his appreciation of things worth while, of the values to which these things are related; if he loses desire to apply what he has learned, and above all, loses the ability to exact meaning from his future experiences as they occur?[18]

Notes

1. Walter Feinberg, *What Is a Public Education and Why We Need It: A Philosophical Inquiry into Self-Development, Cultural Commitment, and Public Engagement* (Lanham: Lexington Books, 2016), pp. 1–24.
2. Louis Menand, *The Metaphysical Club: A Story of Ideas in America* (New York: Farrar, Straus and Giroux, 2002) provides an excellent treatment of how the War contributed to the pragmatic temperament.
3. John Dewey, "My Pedagogical Creed," *School Journal*, 54 (January 1897), pp. 77–80.
4. Charles Taylor, *A Secular Age* (Cambridge: Harvard University Press, 2007), p. 146.
5. Takeo Doi, *The Anatomy of Dependence*, trans. John Bester (Tokyo: Kodansha International, 1971), p. 12.
6. Ibid., p. 51.

7. Taylor, *A Secular Age*, p. 172.
8. Lawrence A. Cremin, *The Transformation of the Schools: Progressivism in American Education, 1876–1956* (New York: Vintage Books, 1961), p. 353.
9. "Vermont Medical School Says Goodbye to Lectures," *All Things Considered*, www.npr.org/sections/health-shots/2017/08/03/541411275/vermont-medical-school-says-goodbye-to-lectures accessed August 4, 2017.
10. Nel Noddings, *Caring: A Feminist Approach to Ethics and Moral Education* (Berkeley, CA: University of California Press, 1986), p. 179.
11. D. C. Phillips, *A Companion to John Dewey's Democracy and Education* (Chicago: University of Chicago Press, 2016).
12. Richard Rorty, *Philosophy and the Mirror of Nature* (Princeton: Princeton University Press, 1979).
13. Hilary Putnam, *Pragmatism* (Oxford: Blackwell, 1995).
14. The University recently decided to close the Center.
15. *Pierce, Governor of Oregon, et al. v. Society of the Sisters of the Holy Names of Jesus and Mary*, 268 U.S. 510 (1925).
16. *West Virginia State Board of Education v. Barnette*, 319 U.S. 624 (1943).
17. Philip W. Jackson, *What Is Education* (Chicago: University of Chicago Press, 2012).
18. As quoted in ibid., p. 41.

2

INFLUENCES ON DEWEY AND THE DEVELOPMENT OF PRAGMATISM[1]

Introduction

John Dewey was a key figure in that distinctly American school of philosophy known as pragmatism. Pragmatism arose after the Civil War and included Charles S. Peirce and William James, among others. After being eclipsed by other philosophical movements, today pragmatism is experiencing a revival in the work of philosophers such as Hilary Putnam, Richard Rorty, Cornell West, Eddie S. Glaude Jr., Robert Brandom and others. Dewey was also a major figure in the progressive education movement, which flourished in the early to middle twentieth century, and he is arguably the single most important American philosopher of education. Dewey was among a handful of preeminent philosophers whose opinions on the events of the day mattered. He was a public intellectual whose ideas about such diverse topics as War and peace, women's suffrage, the Great Depression, capitalism, civil liberties, academic freedom and educational reform received wide attention.

As this suggests, Dewey was more than an armchair philosopher or a disconnected educational theorist, and he was much more than a pundit. He was, perhaps more than any of these, even before the term was coined, a public intellectual who took on the issues of his day, such as war, depression and immigration, addressing them in the popular media as well as in academic publications. He was a philosopher who was willing to get his hands dirty and enter into the fray of political and social debate.

And get his hands dirty he surely did. He was an internationalist who traveled in and wrote about Turkey, the Soviet Union, Japan and China at a time of great social upheaval. He was a social reformer who assisted Jane Addams, promoted labor unions and participated in and helped found the National Association for the Advancement of Colored People (NAACP) and the American Association of University Professors (AAUP). He served as President of the American Philosophical Association (APA) as well as of the American Psychological Association (APA). And in the 1930s, he headed the commission to investigate the charges against the dissident communist leader, Leon Trotsky.

Traces of his influence continue to be present, sometimes in the most unexpected ways. For example, he and his wife raised seven children, and one of his granddaughters, Alice Greeley Dewey, who taught anthropology at the University of Hawaii, was the dissertation advisor of Ann Dunham, Barack Obama's mother. Obama's frequent remark "reality has a way of biting back" could have been coined by Dewey. The remark itself is indicative of the pragmatic view that regardless of what we may hope for, want or believe, the environment, both natural and social, has its way of informing us of our limits.

Early Life

Dewey was born in 1859, the same year Darwin's *Origin of Species* was published and one year before the Civil War began. Both events would prove to be landmarks for Dewey's thought. The *Origin of Species*, Dewey observed, overthrew the traditional conception of "the superiority of the fixed and final," and it enabled him to reject the idea, traceable as far back as Plato and Aristotle, that permanence was perfection and change was a defect. As Dewey noted in his 1910 essay on Darwin, "*the Origin of Species* introduced a mode of thinking that ... was bound to transform the logic of knowledge, and hence the treatment of morals, politics, and religion."[2]

The Civil War was important to the development of his philosophy in a different way. Its conclusion broadened the idea of democracy, setting the stage for the struggle over equal rights, a struggle that has yet to be satisfactorily concluded, and served to reveal the tension between the idea of a more inclusive democracy and that of unrestrained capitalism. Dewey argued that unbridled capitalism is inconsistent with democracy. Today he would be labeled a democratic socialist, but this label, accurate as it is, overemphasizes the political context and occludes the cultural and educational ones that Dewey thought critical to a democratic spirit. Granted, he believed in the need for large-scale social planning, but he also believed that democratic planning on any level must include participation from all stakeholders.

The post-Civil War period was also instrumental in the effort to turn people's attention away from the differences of the past, North v. South, free v. slave, to the possibilities of the future. This change is expressed in the simple shift from the "United States of America" as a plurality as illustrated in the Constitution by "[t]reason against the United States, shall consist only in levying war against *them*" (italics mine) to Lincoln's Gettysburg address: "Now we are engaged in a great civil war to determine whether *that* nation . . . can long endure" (italics mine). Before the War, the term United *States* is said to have signified a plurality—"The United States of America are . . ." After the War and after some fits and starts, it became a singular noun—"The United States of America is . . ." The post–Civil War project's task was to reconstruct a nation that corresponded to the singular noun. Pragmatism was a part of this project, as was progressive education, and Dewey was one of its primary educational architects.

Dewey was as much an American philosopher as Walt Whitman was an American poet or Mark Twain an American humorist. As a man, Dewey reflected his time and place, both their possibilities and their limitations. As a philosopher and educational theorist, he promoted democracy, at least as he understood it at the time—or, to say it somewhat differently—as the times permitted *him* to see it. (The difference in locution concerns the way *we* see the past and how the past comes to be understood in the future.) As a public intellectual, he identified the practices that would promote the ideal of a plurality contained within "one nation indivisible."

Dewey: Early History and Influences

Dewey's writings are best understood in relation to the dramatic social transformation that was beginning even before he was born and that the Civil War temporarily interrupted. Ten years before his birth, railroads first connected the East Coast to the Great Lakes, and a decade later, they were extended to reach from the East Coast to the West. Before he died, a message could be transmitted overseas by telegraph, radio waves and phone, roads connected different part of the country and transcontinental jet air travel was poised to become commonplace. He was a philosopher of this transformation, living through and commenting on two world wars, three depressions and a great wave of immigration; he saw the country altered from a minor player on the international stage to the most powerful nation on earth. Dewey's ideas reflected these changes as he strove to understand their implications for philosophy, for education and for everyday life.

As important as the Civil War was in the rebirth of the nation, Dewey believed that it had not fulfilled the Revolution's promise to democracy. Certainly, the times bore this out. Women could not yet vote, industrial workers were severely exploited, immigrants were victimized discriminated against and Negros (sic) continued to be oppressed and terrorized.

Like Karl Marx (1818–1883), the founder of communism, Dewey felt the new industrial age provided liberating possibilities, and like Marx too, Dewey understood that there were many roadblocks to this advancement that needed to be addressed. These ranged from the anti-scientific and anti-democratic views promoted by some religions as well as the pointless quest for certainty found in the traditional philosophy of the time. It also included the mind-deadening practices of the schools and the selfish exploitation of labor, including child labor, by monopoly capital. Yet unlike Marx, Dewey believed these roadblocks could be removed, not by violent revolution, but by reform guided by scientific methods, experimentation and led by a dedicated corps of knowledgeable intelligent teachers.

He believed that educational transformation was a key to progressive social change.

Dewey's Early Career and the Development of His Thought

Dewey himself had attended public school in Burlington Vermont and then the University of Vermont, where he became interested in philosophy. After graduation, he taught briefly in Oil City, Pennsylvania, where in the 1850s, oil had been discovered and the oil industry in America started. Dewey received his doctorate from Johns Hopkins University in 1884, where he studied under the neo-Hegelian G. Sylvester Morris and at the time was heavily influenced by Hegelian idealism.

Hegelian idealism held that the universe could be understood as a unified, purposeful organic developing whole, striving to overcome apparent contradictions or tensions through ever increasing levels of self-consciousness. Hegel saw human history as a predetermined unfolding of an already present destiny. While the end of this unfolding was only partially understood by humans, it was fully known, from the point of view of the Absolute, or God or a God-perspective.

According to the popular view of Hegel, from the point of view of the Absolute, or God, all human suffering has a larger purpose, but that purpose is not known until after the fact. Wisdom is a product of afterthought. As Hegel famously put it: "The owl of Minerva spreads its wings only with the falling of the dusk." Hegel's view is similar to that of some theologians who insist that human suffering has a larger purpose, a view that has great difficulty explaining surd evils, such as devastating earthquakes, volcanic eruptions, killer tornados, tsunamis or hurricanes. Still, even if humans cannot know the ultimate end, Hegel believed that philosophers like himself could glimpse the dialectical process through which progress toward the Absolute occurs. Although Dewey largely left Hegel's ideas behind as he developed his own, he arguably never completely abandoned a dialectical way of thinking, albeit his was an open one, where possibilities remained underdetermined and where human effort counted. Thus, Dewey replaced Hegel's view that change is purposeful with Darwin's view that change is a random process, but he added that humans can make a difference in the direction evolution takes. In other words, he embraced a more open-ended understanding of change than Hegel. The end is not predetermined by God or "the Absolute," but by humans guided by imagination and inquiry and engaged in cooperative action.

The Pragmatic Turn

Under the influence of older pragmatists, such as C. S. Peirce (1839–1914) and William James (1842–1910), and of Dewey's contemporaries, Jane Addams (1860–1935) and George Herbert Mead (1863–1931), Dewey embraced a thoroughly humanistic point of view, one where humans, not God, served as the principle agent, and where scientific inquiry, not some deterministic dialectic, served as the primary instrument of change and possible progress.

There is some debate about whether Dewey remained a theist in any reasonable sense. The horrendous bloodshed of the Civil War where both sides believed God was on their side likely was likely a factor in his failure to accept his mother's deep Calvinist faith, and it may well have played a subconscious role in his disillusionment with Hegel's theistic conception of evolution. Questions about the existence of God, as distinct from questions about the function of religion, ceased to interest him in any professional way. Instead, Dewey brought Hegel's stairway-to-the-Absolute down to earth, married it to the social sciences and adopted a functional approach to values and their embodiment in institutions like education. The break with Hegel also marked the pragmatic turn and the growing influence of William James and C. S. Peirce, the two towering pragmatists of the time, on Dewey's philosophy.

Early Pragmatism and Its Influence on Dewey

American Pragmatism began as response to rapid changes in American society in the post-Civil War period, emphasizing science, especially the new field of statistics, and deemphasizing *traditional* religion and metaphysics.[3] Pragmatism broke from accepted philosophy by rejecting what Dewey called "the Quest for Certainty" and by denying that truth could be construed as a claim where some inner mental event or image—an idea—corresponded to an external reality, some particular thing. Rather, truth, or what Dewey would refer to as warranted assertability (WA), begins as a disturbance in our habitual way of relating to the world, which is then refined by a careful inquiry that leads to a conclusion that effectively guides future activity. The fact that such conclusions are potentially open to further inquiry and to change leads Dewey to refer to them not as *true* but rather as *warranted assertable propositions* (WA). They are guides that enable us to function effectively.

Pragmatism was also a response to changes in the concept of science from certainty to probability and the development of statistical methods.[4] For the pragmatist, a belief is warranted if it is well justified by reasonable methods of inquiry and supports reasonably secure expectations and productive action. The implication of translating the concept of truth into the notion of WA is to shift the emphasis from conclusion to process and to emphasize the importance of controlled and open inquiry. "The 'settlement' of a particular situation by a particular inquiry is no guarantee that settled conclusions will always remain settled."[5] Logic, then, might be described as inquiry into the process of inquiry.

Pragmatists rejected both the rationalist and the empiricist understanding of knowledge or what some call "true" belief. For while rationalists and empiricists differed about whether thinking was largely a rational deductive process, as exemplified by Descartes, or an empirical associative and inductive process, as exemplified by Locke, both accepted the idea that thought was something that occurred inside the head and that truth was some kind of correspondence between the ideas inside the head and the reality outside it. For Locke, truth was a belief that corresponds to reality. For Descartes, a true belief was one that rested on a logically indubitable foundation of belief—"I think, therefore I am"—and that indicated a similar correspondence.

For the pragmatist, a belief is not something in your head. It is, as Bredo notes, "a willingness to act with regard to the consequences that a claim suggests."[6] Hence, truth is not just the correspondence of our claims about the world with the world itself. As the late Richard Rorty (1931–2007) noted: "questions that require one to climb outside of one's head to see if the beliefs inside correspond to reality outside should not be asked."[7]

For Dewey, thinking is an act of our entire being and does not just occur in some *secret* place called mind. Mind is neither a thing nor a place. It is a process that involves caring and inquiring. It involves the particular ways in which we relate to the world, including the world of other human beings. Mind is shorthand for intelligent inquiry or minding. The phrase "out of your mind" indicates an act based on unintelligent inquiry or on no inquiry. To *mind* something is to attend to that process of inquiry: to make inquiry systematic.

The humorist Stephen Colbert's term "truthiness" is meant to suggest claims that are issued with the tone of truth, but that are counter to all reasonable evidence. Truth, or Dewey's WA, refers to minded beliefs, beliefs that have been subject to careful inquiry and that we have good reason to act on. Since warrants may change due to new experience or better evidence this implies that a truth claim is always tentative. To understand one of the educational implications of this is to understand much about Dewey's educational philosophy. In the rapidly changing world, many old habits become dysfunctional. An important task of education, then, is to develop citizens who, when problematic situations arise, have the capacity and the courage to reflect on old habits and to inquire into the possibility for the formation of new, more productive avenues of conduct.

A problematic situation occurs when the normal flow of experience is disrupted, giving rise to hesitation in action or doubt. Doubt then is initiated by this interruption in our habitual response and is defined as the absence of belief—or a hesitation in the application of a routine to a situation. It is not, however, just a subjective mental state. Rather, it is a conflict or hesitation in action. It entails an interruption in the flow of activity as a result of an irritation, which is experienced as uncertainty. Thought is the name given to an active "investigation directed toward bringing to light further facts which serve" to support one or another course of action that will overcome the disruption.[8] Thinking begins when there is a choice to be made and avenues are uncertain. It includes imagining alternative responses and rehearsing possible ways we might overcome resistance and reinstate the flow of experience.

Thinking is what we do when we want to find a way to reengage with the world.[9] The difference between humans and animals is not to be found, as Aristotle and other philosophers claimed, in our capacity to reason. We are not just *rational* animals. We are also rational *animals*. In other words, we are animals that develop habits and that reflect on them, or at least that are capable of doing so. "We are animals who can act with regard to the meaning of our own behavior."[10]

A belief, as Peirce put it, describes a habit that we are willing to act on. Reason, then, is best understood not as some divine gift, but as a *tool, an instrument* that enables us to solve problems, to renew experience and to get on with life. It is not clear that we are the only animals that can do this, but our capacity to construct and understand symbols certainly allows us to do it for a wider range of purposes than other species.

Thinking, then, entails both a conservative and a liberating element. It is liberating in so far as it projects ways of acting to resolve difficulties and selects what appears to be the most promising of them to remove obstacles, hence facilitating the renewal of experience. We learn through inquiry how actions and consequences relate and use this learning to alter future experience. Thinking also is conservative in so far as it connects and evaluates these alternatives not only by how well they remove the roadblock but also by how well a proposed innovation fits with or preserves the larger network of other habits. Beliefs are, as Peirce observed, habits that we are willing to act on and each one of our beliefs exists in a network of other beliefs. If the new belief is too radically different from the existing network of beliefs, it is in danger of being rejected because it would serve to paralyze action by placing too many habits into conflict with each other. This is one important marker between pragmatism and positivism, the philosophy that makes a sharp *categorical* distinction between analytic truths, or claims that it holds are true by definition (e.g. $1 + 1 = 2$) and synthetic truths, or claims that it holds are true by virtue of experience (e.g. there is one chair in this room). Pragmatists hold that this distinction as made by positivists is too hard and fast.

For the pragmatist, this distinction between analytic and synthetic, while useful on some level, ultimately breaks down. As W. V. Quine (1908–2000) argued,[11] "analytic" truths like $2 + 2 = 4$ are simply those beliefs upon which many of our other beliefs depend. To change them would be to upset a vast network of other beliefs and could render life unmanageably difficult to navigate. Yet there are times when historically such beliefs do undergo change, as, for example, when the parallel postulate in Euclidean geometry was successfully challenged leading to the invention of new, non-Euclidean ways of representing space.

The Ups and Downs of Pragmatism

Pragmatism flourished from the end of the 1800s until the 1950s, when it came into disfavor among American philosophers who, looking to ground their discipline on an independent and more scientifically relevant foundation, turned to linguistic or analytic philosophy, a movement developed mostly in Britain. These philosophers argued that the distinctive role of philosophy was to advance our understanding of language and its use. They dismissed Dewey as too vague and not sufficiently rigorous. However, pragmatism, and especially Dewey, remained in vogue in philosophy of education until the early 1970s, when it too was eclipsed for a while by British analytic philosophy and later by feminism, critical theory and post-modernism. As mentioned earlier, recently, pragmatism and Dewey have experienced a remarkable recovery in both philosophy and philosophy of education.

The Civil War and the Pragmatic Temperament

On the page facing the title of his excellent book on the roots of Pragmatism, *The Metaphysical Club*,[12] Louis Menand placed a drawing by William James of his brother Wilky as he sleeps, recovering from wounds received in the battle of Fort Wagner in 1863. The American Civil War was critical for the development of what I will here call the pragmatic temperament, by which I mean the pragmatist's tendency to explore different alternatives with an eye toward clarifying meaning and commitment and renewing wholeness and activity. This temperament rejects large ideological systems where everything fit into a grand scheme, as well as any philosophical or religious system that discourages or blocks inquiry. It also promotes ameliorative rather than violent social change wherever and whenever possible.

The Civil War and its aftermath wove a deep yet implicit commitment into the American psyche and arguably into American pragmatism, a commitment that continued to define the social imaginary for better part of the twentieth century. Philosophers like Dewey were speaking to, and wanting to speak for a certain kind of nation, one that was unified, pluralistic, tolerant, progressive and hopeful. The temperament of Pragmatism, while rejecting grand schemes, absolutes and ideologies, held firm to a vision of the promise of the American nation as progressive, pluralistic and experimental. The first aspect of this temperament, the rejection of grand schemes, became a formal and well-developed part of the pragmatist moral and educational ideas. The second part, a belief in the possibility of progress and in America as embodying this possibility was forcefully expressed by Dewey when he wrote after the American entry into World War One: "We need to recover something of the militant faith of our forefathers that America is a great idea, and add to it an ardent faith in our capacity to lead the world to see what this idea means as a model for its own future well-being."[13] He failed to see the irony in promoting America as a grand scheme in its own right. Pragmatists did not claim that progress was inevitable, but they believed that it was more likely to happen in America than anywhere else. In this sense, they accepted the idea of American exceptionalism.

Peirce and James on Ideas

Pragmatism is known as a philosophy of action,[14] but as Dewey molded it into a well-developed social and educational philosophy, it is a philosophy of *intelligent—might one even say "prudent"*—action, motivated by impulse, but certainly not impulsive. The role of thought is to mediate between impulse and action in order to make the latter more intelligent and to refine the former. I will return to this in the next chapter, but for now I want to look closely at why pragmatism is understood as a philosophy of action, and what that does and does not mean. Here, we come back to Peirce and James and their formative role in the construction of the pragmatic philosophy.

James defined pragmatism as a way to settle disputes about truth, and meaning: "the tangible fact at the root of all our thought-distinctions, however subtle, is that there is no one of them so fine as to consist in anything but a possible difference of practice."[15] Or, "Consider what conceivable effects of a practical kind the object may involve . . . Our conception of those effects . . . is then for us the whole of our conception of the object."[16] If there is no practical difference, then there is no distinction to be made, the meaning is the same, and if there is no distinction to be made, then issues of the truth of the one verses the truth of the other cannot arise.

For James, truth is not static. "Truth happens to an idea. It *becomes* true, is made true by events."[17] Dewey expresses a similar point about meaning when he proclaimed: "consequences not antecedents supply meaning."[18] The view that meaning and truth (not exactly the same things) depend on future events or consequences is one of the more controversial aspects of pragmatism. For example, the philosopher Bertrand Russell rejected this view of truth, arguing that: "If truth, . . . depends on the future, then in so far as it is in our power to alter the future, it is in our power to alter what should be asserted." Russell continues: "Did Caesar cross the Rubicon? I should determine an affirmative answer as unalterably determined by a past event." (That is, that Caesar really did cross the Rubicon.)[19]

Russell misses some of the important nuances of the pragmatic view. Dewey's concern is about what we are "warranted" in asserting. Given that we do not have direct access to the past, Dewey would likely say about Russell's example that we are warranted in affirming that Caesar crossed the Rubicon because the evidence for the claim is overwhelming. Yet it is always possible that evidence could arise which puts the claim into question.

James's emphasis was somewhat different. Sometimes he seemed to hold that if we believe something strongly enough, then we will act on that belief, thus increasing its likelihood of impacting our experience. This would then serve to change not only he nature of a truth claim, but the facts of the case as well—the way the world really is. This is one of the points he seems to make in his religious writings, but there are other possible examples.[20] Consider how our monetary system depends on belief. It works largely because most of us, most of the time, believe it will work and thus we act on this belief, and, by doing so, we make it a true belief. If enough people cease to believe the system will work, then it will fail. It will become untrue. Such an example would seem to support James's claim that "There are, then, cases where a fact cannot come at all unless a preliminary faith exists in its coming. *And where faith in a fact can help create the fact.*"[21] At other times, he promotes a more contentious interpretation, one where our beliefs are true if they contribute to a more harmonious or more comfortable life.[22]

There is another consideration that I will address in the last chapter. When the context in which an event has been embedded changes, we are often justified in re-describing past truths in a way that takes into account our changing understanding. In a narrow sense, the truth claim does not change, but its expression does.

I will come back to the question of the nature of historical truth in the last chapter, but for now, it is useful to note that Peirce's view of truth is closer to Russell's at this point than it is to Dewey's and certainly to James's. Peirce held out for an ultimate reality that could be described by a hypothetical and long-term scientific consensus. He had a very strong reaction to his friend and benefactor James, writing to him that "I thought your Will to Believe was a very exaggerated utterance, such as injures a serious man very much."[23]

Peirce on Truth and Science

Peirce's ultimate philosophical bête Noir was Rene Descartes (1598–1650), the French philosopher who insisted that through systematic doubt we could reach an indubitable truth. For Peirce, Descartes had set an impossible task for philosophy—to prove existence through systematic doubt until the point was reached when doubt was no longer possible, when all possible contradiction had been eliminated, and certainty reached.

For Peirce and the pragmatists who followed him, Descartes's entire exercise was academic, largely beside the point and self-refuting. Doubt, Peirce reminded us, is not something we normally undertake intentionally. We become aware of our beliefs when things start to go wrong. Rather doubt is something that comes upon us when our normal platform of beliefs, often taken for granted, is shaken, as, for example, it had been during Descartes time by the Thirty Years' religious war (1618–1648). Descartes may have *feigned* to doubt the existence of the quill that he used to write but not enough to stop writing. And he never seemed to doubt the stable construction of the bed upon which he did much of his thinking and writing.

Peirce argues that we hold most of our beliefs unconsciously, acting on them but not consciously aware that we hold them. Whenever I climb the stairs to my study, take a walk, fry an egg, I am taking for granted a certain kind of world. One where stairs do not usually collapse, where the earth is stable and able to support me and where the fire I light can be controlled. Doubt arises in a specific circumstance and for a specific reason. Although some philosophers still insist that Peirce missed Descartes point—that he was affirming not doubt, but the *possibility* of doubt—the *point had been made*, and the "quest for certainty," or for an indubitable foundation, as Dewey would come to call it, never again enjoyed quite the same *unchallenged* philosophical status.

For Peirce as well as for Dewey, Descartes's mistake was to think of belief and doubt as a state of a *subjective* mind rather than a state of engagement. As a state of engagement belief in X means that: *I have confidence that X*. For Peirce, "*confidence that X*" is shorthand for something else—a habit of action. If I say that I believe in the brakes of my car I mean that if I want to stop I will depress the pedal. This confidence is a habit, one that I can draw upon when I need to slow down the car. For Peirce, doubt is "not a habit but the privation of a habit."[24] Anticipating Dewey, Peirce continues: "A privation of a habit . . . must be a condition of erratic activity that in some way must get superseded by a habit."[25] When I doubt the existence of something, what I am doing is entertaining the possibility that that thing has no reality in this world or that it will not work in the way I normally expect it to. To doubt my brakes is to consider the possibility that when I need to stop they may not work. If I am already driving, it means that rather than pushing the brake pedal alone, and, finding it failing, I will try to shift to a lower gear or find some other way to slow down. Inquiry is defined as a struggle to resolve doubt. Trying a lower gear is a kind of inquiry, even if we do this instantaneously, without conscious thought.

Some Peirce scholars will rightly object that the example of the brakes on a car fits James more than it does Peirce, giving Peirce more of a practical inflection than is justified. This is not to say that Peirce's work did not have important practical applications. He is credited with the development of many aspects of statistics, and in one famous court case, he and his father Benjamin, testifying as expert witnesses, used their newly developed statistical techniques to support a charge of forgery.[26] In addition, Peirce's work for the US Coast Survey likely had important practical ramifications. Still, Peirce did not believe that real science was motivated by practical concerns but rather was motivated by "a single-minded absorption in the search (for knowledge) for its own sake—a single-mindedness that forgets every theory the moment the facts of observation appear against it."[27]

Besides reshaping the aim of philosophical inquiry from a quest for certainty to a struggle to resolve doubt and to fix habit through inquiry, Peirce held that scientific laws should not be understood as absolute determinants of behavior, but as tools or instruments that cannot be ignored and must be considered if we want to successfully arrest doubt. Science does not fix behavior, it liberates it.

Dewey's Reinterpretation of Darwin

Dewey picked up this idea of science as liberating in his reinterpretation of Darwin. In 1909, Dewey addressed the profound influence of Darwin on human thought. "Philosophy forswears inquiry after absolute origins and absolute finalities in order to explore specific values and the specific conditions that generate them."[28] Unlike many who believed that Darwin supported determinism or feared that Darwin undercut the props of civilized society, Dewey found in Darwin the basis for a new way of thinking about human agency and responsibility.

> The new logic introduces responsibility into the intellectual life. To idealize and rationalize the universe at large is after all a confession of inability to master the courses of things that specifically concern us. As long as mankind suffered from this impotency, it naturally

shifted a burden of responsibility that it could not carry over to the more competent shoulders of the transcendent cause. But if insight into specific conditions of value and into specific consequences of ideas is possible, philosophy must in time become a method of locating and interpreting the more serious of the conflicts that occur in life, and a method of projecting ways for dealing with them: a method of moral and political diagnosis and prognosis.[29]

Not everyone would agree with this assessment. Besides the objections of deep-seated religious literalists who believed Darwin was doing the work of the Devil, there were the unbridled Social Darwinists who believed that any government intervention to promote human improvement was bound to fail or prolong the lives of unfit practices and people. For the Social Darwinist, competition and cruel struggle were the main ingredients in the improvement of the species. Unbridled competition eliminated the weak and enabled the strong to survive and reproduce. To Dewey, the Social Darwinists were apologists for the rise of industrial capitalism and the robber barons who controlled it. For them, the natural order dictated that the working class was to be isolated and controlled from above and any attempt to organize workers was to be discouraged, by force if necessary.

In contrast, Dewey promoted social cooperation as the main source of species development. Much influenced by Jane Addams and his own wife Alice, Dewey found classical capitalism and the social Darwinism that supported it an *uncreative* and destructive force in so far as the social good was concerned. Later in the twentieth century he would reject Marxism, at least as he understood it, as overly deterministic, and its political manifestation, orthodox communism, as authoritarian and anti-democratic.

In contrast to the destructive competition fostered by social Darwinists like Herbert Spencer in England and Charles Sumner in the United States, Dewey emphasized the benefits of cooperation, democratic planning and coordinated social action. Dewey held that human cooperation was essential in controlling nature and advancing the survival of the species, and he saw ethical ideals, such as love, charity etc., although changeable in expression, as a kind of codification of practices that have proved critical in species survival and development.[30] In contrast to the social Darwinist, who argued that progress came about through the culling of the weakest and enabling the survival of the fittest, an argument against any kind of systematic welfare, Dewey held that by looking after the most helpless we develop group survival traits, such loyalty, solidarity, the ability and willingness to care for all members.[31]

Dewey as a Public Intellectual

Peirce and James prepared much of the ground for Dewey's pragmatism, while Dewey both deepened its philosophical basis and extended its insights beyond philosophy to the social, political, aesthetic and educational realms. This was consistent with the tenor of pragmatism, but even more, it reflected Dewey's belief that philosophy should not just address the problems of philosophers, as he believed had been the preoccupation of past philosophers. To do so was to make philosophy sterile, irrelevant and overly academic. Rather, philosophy's concern must be the problems of men.[32] Traditional philosophy's quest for certainty and absolute truth was to be abandoned and replaced by whatever science, or intellectual inquiry, will allow us to claim and for however long it will allow us to claim it.

Thus, Dewey's educational and social philosophy are directly linked to his unique understanding of both science and democracy and to the possibilities that he believed they held for enhancing the lives of people. For Dewey, the importance of science was more than its conclusions. Science was both a way of thinking and a way of being, each essential to democracy. As a way of thinking, science was a method to reflect on and refine belief and to improve individual experience and social life. As a way of being, science involved a community engaged in reflective thought and experimental practice, where evidence is public and available for all to see and where a careful consideration of evidence is used to decide differences and formulate consensus. A major task of philosophy was to make these methods self-conscious and to promote their extension from the natural to the social realm. A major task of education would be to promote these methods across generations.

Notes

1. Parts of this chapter are drawn from my essay "Dewey, John" in D. C. Phillips, *Encyclopedia of Educational Theory and Philosophy* (Los Angeles: Sage), pp. 223–228.
2. John Dewey, *The Influence of Darwin on Philosophy and other Essays* (New York: Henry Holt & Co., 1919), p. 1.
3. Louis Menand, *The Metaphysical Club: A Story of Ideas in America* (New York: Farrar, Straus and Giroux, 2001).
4. Ibid., pp. 177–201.
5. John Dewey, *Logic: The Theory of Inquiry* (New York: Henry Holt & Co., 1938), p. 8.
6. Eric Bredo, unpublished paper on Peirce's conception of meaning. Email correspondence September 9, 2017.
7. Quoted in ibid.
8. John Dewey, *How We Think* (Buffalo: Promethean Books, 1991), p. 9.
9. Putting aside the dualistic heuristic used by the author, a modern version of this view can be found in Daniel Kahneman, *Thinking Fast and Slow* (New York: FarrarStraus and Giroux, 2011).

10. Bredo, op. cit.
11. Willard Van Orman Quine, *From A Logical Point of Vie* (Cambridge: Harvard University Press, 1950).
12. Louis Menand, *The Metaphysical Club: A Story of Ideas in America* (New York: Farrar, Sraus and Giroux, 2001).
13. John Dewey, *The Middle Works of John Dewey*, V.11 1918–1919, *Essays*(Carbondale: Southern Illinois University Press, 2003), http://pm.nlx.com.proxy2.library.illinois.edu/xtf/search?sort=&keyword=We+need+to+recover+something+of+the+militant+faith+of+our+forefathers+that+America+is+a+great+idea%2C+and+add+to+it+an+ardent+faith+in+our+capacity+to+lead+the+world+to+see+what+this+idea+means+as+a+model+for+its+own+future+well-being&ctitle=Dewey%3A+Collected+Works+%281st+Release%29&brand=default
14. Peter Godfrey-Smith, "Pragmatism: Philosophical Aspect," J. Wright (ed.), *International Encyclopedia of the Social and Behavioral Sciences*, 2nd edition, Vol. 18 (Oxford: Elsevier, 2015), pp. 803–807.
15. William James, "What Pragmatism Means," *Pragmatism and the Meaning of Truth* (Cambridge: Harvard University Press, 1978), p. 29. Here James was largely following Peirce in his 'How to Make our Ideas Clear'.
16. Ibid., p. 29.
17. William James, *Pragmatism and the Meaning of Truth* (Cambridge: Harvard University Press, 1975), p. 97.
18. "Experience and Nature," *The Collected Works of John Dewey: The Later Works, Vol. 1: 1925* (Carbondale: Southern Illinois University Press, 2008), p. 124.
19. As quoted in D. C. Phillips, *A Companion to John Dewey's Democracy and Education* (Chicago: University of Chicago Press, 2016), p. 125.
20. William James, *The Will to Believe and Other Essays in Popular Philosophy* (Cambridge: Harvard University Press, 1979).
21. William James, *Will to Believe and other Essays in Popular Philosophy* (Gutenberg ebook 26659, May 8, 2009), www.gutenberg.org/files/26659/26659-h/26659-h.htm, p. 25.
22. Cheryl Misak, *The American Pragmatists* (Oxford: Oxford University Press, 2013), p. 63.
23 Cheryl Misak, *The American Pragmatists* (Oxford: Oxford University Press, 2013), p. 64.
24. Charles S. Peirce, *Values in a Universe of Chance: Selected Writings (1839–1914)*, ed. Philip P. Wiener (New York: Doubleday Anchor Books, 1958), p. 189.

25. Ibid.
26. Menand, *The Metaphysical Club*, pp. 163–176.
27. C. S. Peirce, "Lessons of the History of Science," Philip P. Weiner (ed.), *Values in a Universe of Chance: Selected Writings of Charles S. Peirce 1839–1914* (New York: Doubleday Anchor Books, 1959), pp. 227–228.
28. John Dewey, *The Middle Works*, Vol. 4 (1907–1919) (Carbondale: Southern Illinois University Press, 2003), p. 11.
29. Ibid., p. 14.
30. Appreciation to Eric Bredo and our unpublished correspondence for this wording.
31. John Dewey, *The Early Works of John Dewey*, Vol. 5 (1895–1898) (Carbondale: Southern Illinois University Press, 2003), p. 35.
32. John Dewey, *Problems of Men* (New York: Philosophical Library, 1946).

3

DEWEY'S PHILOSOPHY

Introduction

Dewey's writings are extensive, covering many different topics occupying more than a shelf on my study. They are also available on line[1] sponsored by the Dewey Center at Southern Illinois University at Carbondale. Dewey wrote on philosophy, psychology, ethics, art, politics, economics, democracy and education, among other topics. He addressed issues of war and peace, immigration and women's suffrage, logic and scientific inquiry, to mention only a few. To focus on education alone to the neglect of others is to run the risk of distortion and misunderstand. Dewey's educational philosophy is intricately tied to his thoughts on psychology, politics and art. Woven through all of these fields is his distinctive understanding of the meaning of meaning, and in this chapter, I use this understanding to examine different elements of his philosophy.

Dewey's idea of meaning links the disparate elements of his philosophy. For example, to the extent that Dewey embraces aspects of child-centered education, it is because he believed it could provide an educational experience where meaning will continue to grow for each child and where a democratic community could develop. To the extent that Dewey is committed to democracy, it is because he believed that democracy provides people with meaning, enabling them to reexamine existing ideas and to connect them and develop new ones. To the extent that Dewey values art, it is because it heightens the intensity and meanings of everyday experience and because it contributes "meaning and value to future experience."[2] To the extent that he valued science, it is because he held that it could serve to stabilize and reproduce positive, meaningful experiences.

From Confusion to Order

To understand Dewey's conception of meaning, it is useful to recall William James's famous description of the world of the new infant as one of blooming, buzzing confusion. The infant begins life overwhelmed by experience. The confusion is reduced when the child begins to attend to some stimuli and ignore others as mere noise. Perhaps this is what the Gospel of John means by "in the beginning was the word" and out of the word came order. In any event, a child's initial experience provides the scaffolding upon which more complicated experience is understood. This is one reason for concern when the life and cultural experiences of some group of children is systematically ignored in school.

Consider, for example, how an infant might discover that the object that she is attending to is her own hand. Or, that the yellow circle—the moon—she is reaching for cannot be touched. In each case, the baby is refining her world as she comes to understand experientially that she exists and that she exists at a distance from other things, like the moon, but not from things like the hand in front of her eyes. In reaching for, but not grasping, the moon, she has conducted her first experiment and has come to her first proto conclusion—that there are differences between me and it, between here and there and between now and then. The process of reaching and not grasping is a first step in the critical distinction between self and other. If the infant's world is not quite as confusing as James thought, it is confusing enough.

A major task of Dewey and other pragmatists is to understand how confusion turns to meaningful order, not only for infants, but for all of us. For Dewey, when we understand the meaning of something, we see its connections to other things and to a human purpose. As a result, we function more effectively. The infant may not be able to touch the moon, but she now is beginning to develop important ideas and distinctions—self and other, near and far—and is beginning too to develop the capacity to judge how far she can effectively reach. Here she is implicitly learning about the limits of a reach, as she starts to coordinate an optical percept with a feel percept. This coordination, once learned, is the very basis of meaning.

This example suggests that meaning is a multi-level achievement. Where one level of meaning is crystallized new meanings can be developed, and these new meanings may then serve as means to reflect on the value of older levels. Consider as an example the way in which reaching and seeing are reshaped through sophisticated instruments such as telescopes and space ships.

Speaking About Meaning

There are a number of different ways that we talk about ideas and meaning Sometimes ideas are spoken of as if they were furniture *in* a room. "The ideas that I have in my head." Given this view, a person gains meaning by having more ideas in the head, or mind. The more furniture—ideas—a person has, the fuller the mind. At other times, we may speak of the room as cluttered—I have so many ideas, I can't remember things. The mind is also sometimes spoken of as if it were a mirror and ideas as reflections on the mirror of things in the world outside, as in, "I have an image of the mountain in my head." Here truth is seen as a statement that accurately expresses a correspondence between the image in our head and something outside of it.

For Dewey, these metaphors miss a great deal that is important about the notion of meaning (as well as truth), and they arise out of a problematic conception of the mind, promulgated by philosophers like Locke. Locke proposed that the mind was passive describing it as a tabula rasa. The metaphors also support a misguided understanding of education as the process of filling up the mind with facts.

Given this picture of the mind as a blank slate, ideas were seen as impressions of qualities like red or hard. Some qualities Locke labeled as primary, or as existing independent of mind and outside it. Even though they were independent, they impacted the mind and formed a direct impression on it—as chalk on the blank slate. These qualities include, size, texture, solidarity, motion, rest etc. Other qualities, he labeled secondary qualities. These included color, taste and smell and are qualities that Locke held do not exist in the object but are produced by the mind in accord with certain powers in the object. Locke had a complicated theory about how these impressions were formed. He distinguished primary qualities such as size, shape, motion and solidarity, which he believed the mind could grasp directly, from secondary qualities such as color or sound which he claimed were subjective constructions of the mind. The mind had the capacity then to combine ideas, to compare them and to develop general principles from particular cases.

This view of mind as mainly an effect of the external world had many critics, starting with David Hume (1711–1776), questioning the distinction between primary and secondary qualities. Hume showed this distinction could not explain subtler qualities of mind, such as the idea of causation or even the concept of number. And as George Berkeley (1685–1753) argued earlier, given that we never perceive a primary quality without a secondary one—shape and size without color—Locke's distinction between the two cannot hold. For Dewey, Locke's view of the mind as basically a passive receptacle raised the question how is communication possible. If, in fact, meaning exists in each individual's head, then how do we ever know that we actually mean the same thing when we say, for example, "blue ball"? In other words, how is communication possible? For Dewey, Locke's view of mind and meaning was largely a non-starter. We do in fact communicate, and any theory of mind that does not take that into account needs revision.

Locke's basic error for Dewey was to think of mind as a storage place or slate for ideas and then to classify mind as a noun that connotes some kind of object, like a container. For Dewey, mind is better thought of as a verb, such as in, "Will you mind the store while I step out for a minute?" or as caring for something, as in "mind your sister!" rather than as a noun. Or, as an adverb, such as in, "act mindfully!" The term "mind" for

Dewey indicates not a thing or a place, but a way of relating. To the limited extent that "mind" *serves as* a noun it denotes "the whole system of meanings as they are embedded in the workings of organic life."[3] We become *conscious* of segments of this system when we consider the implications of action, and this may bring into play other aspects of the system of meaning.

Meaning as Function and Connection

Ideas for Dewey are best understood in terms of the response tendencies or plans of action. They are hypothesis about how to achieve aims. Concepts are best understood in terms of fixing use. "Any meaning sufficiently individualized to be directly grasped and readily used, and thus fixed by a word, is a conception."[4] Concepts then are meanings that have been standardized *by use* that serve to reduce the flux of experience, making it intelligible and shaping it into something functional. For example, a small child learns that that place where she hides and plays peek-a-boo—has another function—people sit on it and call it a "chair." Objects that begin as an obscure, vague parts of our background take on their meaning as chairs, tables, lamps etc. as we learn to use them and to signal their use to others. Communication is possible then as an aspect of use and as a result of the formation of concepts. We form a concept of a chair when we know how to use it and can communicate that use to others. Objects come into being through their functions. As Dewey notes:

> The acquisition of definiteness and of coherence (or constancy) of meanings is derived from practical activities. By rolling an object, the child makes its roundness appreciable; by bouncing it, he singles its elasticity; by throwing it, he makes weight its conspicuous

> distinctive factor. Not through the senses, but by means of the reaction, the responsive adjustment is the impression made distinctive, and given a character marked off from other qualities that call out unlike reactions.[5]

Concepts enable us to make connections, to manipulate parts of the world, to put events in a wider context of past and future and to go beyond immediate experience—to make inferences and to imagine something new.

A Contemporary View of Meaning

A different, but still problematic, view of meaning from that of Locke is found in twentieth-century Logical Positivism (LP). LP ties meaning to propositions and the conditions of verification. A statement is meaningful, i.e. has meaning, only if there is some possible condition under which it can be verified. If there is some test by which it can be verified or falsified, it is a meaningful proposition. If there is no conceivable way it can be verified or falsified, it is a *pseudo* proposition.

We can illustrate this through the often-used example of the statement: "The king of France is bald." Although the statement is grammatically correct and fits the form of a proposition, it is meaningless in its present form because there is no king of France. However, the statement could be made meaningful if broken into two parts, i.e. there is a king of France, and he is bald. The first part is false rendering the entire statement false, but it is still meaningful.

For Dewey, the LP view of meaning was exceptionally narrow—something was meaningful for the LP only if it could be verified by sense experience or by logical entailment. LP eliminated all kinds of experiences that people describe as meaningful. "Wow, that was a meaningful book!" or "That was the most meaningful relation I ever had!" or "What do you think the play meant?" or "Just how should we interpret the meaning of the Second Amendment?"

Dewey could agree with part of the logical positivist project. The idea of making our ideas clear by sharpening vague ideas, which involves the "unconscious mixing together of different meanings,"[6] into ones where the different meanings are separated and can be tested is something Dewey could agree with. He would also accept the notion that experience is not just something that happens internally. Experience is objectively manifested through behavior. However, he would not rule out as meaningless aesthetic or other intense experiences, or to reduce them, as LP would suggest, to some observable neurological events, which then could be tested empirically. An example of this kind of reduction would be to translate a statement like "I love you" into an empirically testable claim like "whenever I see you my oxytocin level rises way beyond normal." For Dewey, to make an experience meaningful for the positivists you had to deny the experience by reducing it to something else, and this is crazy. Dewey would look for behavior consistent with "I love you." The lyrics to the song "On the Street Where You live" has a better take on love than a neurological examination.

Finally, there is the view of meaning associated with Descartes, Kant and, more recently, Chomsky that there are intersubjective qualities shared by all humans that make meaning possible. For Descartes, this intersubjective quality is reason and logic modeled after geometry. The prime example for Descartes is the indisputable existence of an *I* and the elaborate system of truths that he believed could be deduced from indisputable self-existence. For Kant, the prime examples are certain ideas that make orderly thought possible, but which cannot be known by experience. These include our notions of causation, time, space and the like, which Kant felt we impose on the initial chaotic experience. For Chomsky, it is innate mental or linguistic structures that enable us to learn language. It involves a universal grammar that transforms human sounds into creative language. While Dewey would likely accept the scientific evidence in support of Chomsky's position, he would want to distinguish between meaning and some of the conditions that make it possible. And he would want to stress the function of meaning as a communicative act.

That Blooming, Budding Confusion Again and Again

To understand Dewey's conception of meaning, think again of James's idea of the infant's blooming, buzzing confusion and think of that blooming, buzzing confusion not as happening just once, but over and over again throughout our lives. Now ask: "What happens when confusion ends?" The quick answer is that things become clearer. But "clearer" is a visual metaphor, and more happens than improved eyesight when confusion ends. Take the following example.

Imagine that you are a passenger in a car (prior to GPS devices) and that you travel the same route every day. However, because you are always engaged in conversation with other passengers, you do not recall exactly how to reach your destination by yourself. Then something happens to the driver, and you have to drive yourself. The first time you have to *drive* the route is unclear to you; some of the landmarks are familiar, but you are uncertain what to do when you reach them. Do you take a right, a left, go straight ahead? Then, after a time or two, you begin to recognize landmarks and use them to guide your way. In other words, things begin to take on meaning in terms of your purpose and their connection to one another. You recognize *that* particular store not just as, say any old drugstore, but also rather as the place where you take a right.

Then, suppose one day your right lane is blocked by construction. Now you need a wider sense of meaning, something like a map, that can help you get to your destination through a different route. But instead of getting a physical map, you begin to reflect on the way various streets are connected, or you make a few mistakes and then develop an orderly alternative route. Streets that you once never noticed now take on new meaning. Now, one might ask: Where does this new meaning exist? Is it in my head? For Dewey, "in my head" is a metaphor. It stands for consequential connections. Turn right, or you get lost! Meaning is a relationship between purpose, action and environment through which purpose is achieved, frustrated or reformulated.

The construction then stands as a literal roadblock that leads us to realize that our old habits are not working, and to stimulate the development of new ones. (Not this right, but the next, then a left and a right etc.) The blooming, buzzing confusion ends once you have a new *end in view* which not only is defined by your ultimate destination but also by the route you need to take to get there. Meaning is not just a matter of "mind," nor is it just a matter of "body." It is a matter of purpose, habit, reflection and the development of new, more effective habits. To know the meaning of a statement is to know the likely consequences of acting on it as if it were true.

When we acquire new meaning, we do so by using some old habits to address new, problematic situations and then to develop new habits. In the earlier example, while you may have been uncertain about how to reach your destination, you still could tell your right from your left; you still knew how to drive and what time you needed to be at your destination. This, of course, is another variation on Peirce's critique of Descartes's conception of doubt. Just as we cannot doubt everything at once, so too we cannot give up all of our habits as we acquire new ones.

Dewey's Ecological Standpoint

When I said earlier that meanings were part of a system for Dewey, I did not want to suggest that this system was only mental, as if it were contained in *something* called the mind which was walled off from another *thing* called the body, and that both together were walled off from something else called nature or the environment. Nor did I mean to suggest that these connections were closed and bounded. They reach beyond themselves and interact with other open systems.

Dewey was an ecologist long before the term was common. The human act of breathing is part of an ecological system that connects us to a larger natural world of symbiotic relations, relations that are illustrated most profoundly in the production and exchange of life-giving gases between humans and plants. This connection is closely tied to Dewey's idea of experience, which he notes "occurs continuously, because the interaction of live creature and environing conditions is involved in the very process of living."[7] It is a transactional approach to organism/environment interaction where interdependence is the key to meaning. We act upon the environment, suffer or enjoy the effects of that action back on us and then act again.

Implications

For Dewey, meaning is grounded in our everyday life experience within both a social and a natural environment. Meaning forms the basis of the communicative engagements that *human* community requires. But again, meaning is not just something esoteric located in the head. Dewey holds that there is an important connection between the idea of meaning and the notion of means. In a limited sense, we can think of meaning somewhat like we think of a tool or instrument. (This is why his philosophy is sometimes called instrumentalism.) The meaning of a hammer has to do with things like nails and wood and with activities like building and fixing. The meaning of a hammer is entailed in all that we can do with it. The idea of meaning then points to the significance of an experience in terms of its consequences. It is grounded in experience, but it also takes us beyond the immediacy of experience by allowing us to make critical inferences. Consider the following contrast that Dewey makes to illustrate this point:

> By habit, by conditioned reflex, hens run to the farmer when he makes a clucking noise, or when they hear the rattle of grain in a pan. When the farmer raises his arms to throw the grain they scatter and fly, to return only when the movement ceases. They act as if alarmed; his movement is thus not a sign of food; it is a stimulus that evokes flight. But a human infant learns to discount such movements; to become interested in them as events preparatory to a desired consummation; he learns to treat them as signs of an ulterior event so that his response is to their meaning. He treats them as means to consequences.[8]

In other words, the difference between the hens and the human in this example is that for the human, the raising of the arm is treated as a part of a larger series of events and not as the event itself. It takes on meaning *as a part* of this larger series and is taken as a sign for something else. It is taken as a *means* to something of consequence.

Now, this very same idea occurs over and over again in Dewey's work but from different angles. In one of his early psychological writings, he addresses the behaviorist's view that something identified as a stimulus exists independent of any meaning of its own[9] and argues this is misleading. He shows that the ongoing activity of the subject determines the meaning of the stimulus for her. A loud noise will mean one thing in a quiet study and quite another on a rifle range. This is one reason why experiments performed in pristine laboratories often cannot be replicated in everyday settings.

In a work on ethics, he shows how positivist philosophers wrongly dismiss the objective character of evaluative statements as merely ejaculatory expressions, like a baby's cry. For Dewey, what they miss is the entire communicative engagement that cry, response and satisfaction entail.[10] The cry is meaningful, not in itself alone, but because of the series of communicative engagements which it initiates and the language development that it anticipates. The meaning is to be found in the exchange between a child and a caregiver. Consider the following chain: A cry indicates a vague, problematic situation. Does it signal hunger or a wet diaper? Response 1. Check diaper; result, diaper is dry. Response 2. Give bottle; result, cry stops, baby gurgles. Caregiver gives warm hug. The meaning is in the interaction between sign, e.g. the cry, the interpretation = hungry/bottle, the consequences of acting on the interpretation = pleasant sounds. For Dewey, meaning begins in experience, adds to that experience and ends in a new experience. The cry indicates a need, the parent interprets the cry as indicating a *specific* need, predicts what will satisfy it, say a bottle, acts on that prediction, provides the bottle, baby is satisfied and goes to sleep. Both baby and parent now begin to see *this* kind of cry having meaning—I am hungry, feed me!

Dewey's idea of meaning assumes a certain kind of world, one which is initially precarious and where the search for meaning is an effort to provide stability, predictability and communicability by establishing a condition for coordination and participation. As Dewey notes:

> Where communication exists, things in acquiring meaning, thereby acquire representatives, surrogates, signs and implicates, which are infinitely more amenable to management, more permanent and more accommodating, than events in their first estate.[11]

Meaning, Communication and Control

The critical aspect of meaning is its role in communication, or the coordination of intentions, means and consequences. Take the farmer throwing the grain in the earlier example. For the hen, the throw is not a communicative act because she cannot coordinate her response with the intention of the farmer. Whereas the farmer intends to indicate with the throw, "eat!" the hen *reacts* to the throw as if it were a threat (without verbalizing or conceptualizing it). Contrast the softball catcher, who is able to understand the meaning of the throw in the same way as the pitcher and to coordinate her response accordingly.

One of the problems with the idea that meaning exists in the head and reflects the world is that meaning is already a part of that world. It is, to appropriate Dewey's terms, "events in their second estate." "Language is a natural function of human association,"[12] and meaning is a critical feature of language. But this goes beyond written or spoken language. Action and gestures, paintings and music are meaningful.

Dewey is most interested in the function of meaning in expanding the control and predictability of human experience[13] and in enabling people to control the connection between an event and the enjoyment or suffering that follows from that event. He uses the example of fire. Before humans learned to make fire it was simply the source of an immediate enjoyment—warmth—or a cause of pain and suffering. In learning to *make* fire and to control it the experiencing of fire became a distinctive, meaningful operation, mediated by reflection. The event of fire of course remains just what it is, as do our feelings about fire—fear, dread, comfort, coziness etc., but when thought intervenes, it enables us to control and regulate both event and feeling and to schedule their occurrence.[14]

Dewey held that there was a critical connection between the ideas of meaning, communication and community. Although many species have some forms of communication—crows can signal existing danger to other crows; young monkeys, kittens, puppies can distinguish threat signs from play signs—the human capacity to share and communicate knowledge across distance and time is rather remarkable and is one of the conditions of education as a process of incorporating shared meaning across space and time.

Recent theorists such as Michael Corballis share Dewey's view that the development of shared meaning is coextensive with and critical for human evolution. With a system of meanings in place we can learn about much of the world second hand.[15] The human child can be told in a way that the chick cannot that the throw is not intended as a threat. Of course, there are considerable differences among scholars as to how *language* arose, whether it is unique to humans and whether it can be explained through orthodox evolutionary theory. However, the connection between meaning, communication and the possibility for complex communal interaction on many levels is hard to deny.

As mentioned earlier, for Dewey, the idea of meaning is connected with the idea of *meaningfulness*. An event is meaningful as a result of a heightened relationship between an immediate happening and its suggested or inferred consequences. An event becomes meaningful precisely to the extent that we can treat it not merely as a stimulus that provokes a response—hot stove=pain=remove hand and yell—but as a signs signaling some other event. Consider the response of a person who is experiencing a sphere coming at her at, say, 75 miles an hour. Most of us would try to duck, but not if the person is that catcher on a softball team mentioned earlier. Rather, she responds not to an uninterpreted stimulus, but to a *pitch*. A pitch is a *social* act that requires the catcher to understand her role, together with having an implicit understanding of the rules of softball, and it requires an understanding that everyone else understands the on-coming sphere in the same way. The game itself provides a context for the meaning of certain acts. It defines the thrown ball as a pitch, not as a weapon—and it stamps its significance—Strike! Out! Game over!

Meaning: A Quest for Wholeness and Control

For Dewey, meaning involves three aspects, not just two. It not only involves an agent—e.g. a speaker or writer and a receiver; e.g. a listener or reader—it also draws on the cultural system that make human sounds and gestures meaningful social events. For Dewey, the quest for meaning is a quest for wholeness within the context of a social system, or as Alexander so aptly puts it: "There is a general impulsion for wholeness in all activity, according to Dewey."[16] This sense of wholeness is most often associated with art and the aesthetic experience. Yet, a truly consummate experience is not limited to artworks. We might observe an important baseball game where our team clinches the pennant and say, "That was a *real* game!" meaning every minute counted and that we were emotionally tied up with watching it from beginning to end. It has the kind of unity that we might experience in a fine drama or by looking at a particularly powerful painting. Experience can be mundane as when we satisfy our hunger with a peanut butter sandwich. Or, it can be profound, like when Fleming realized that the mold on a slice of bread could be used to cure disease. As Dewey put it, "the difference between an adjustment to a physical stimulus and a mental act is that the latter involves response to a thing in its meaning; the former does not."[17]

Dewey is interested in the way meaning mediates, and in how symbols serve to stabilize and control the environment for the sake of human purposes, community and richer experience. Some have interpreted his emphasis on control in nefarious ways, as if control would be at the expense of freedom rather than in the service of it. This takes a considerable stretch. While it is true that Dewey was a strong advocate for the development of a science of human conduct at a time when the social sciences were just starting to develop, he was not arguing for a deterministic view of human nature, nor that social science should be used to blindly manipulate citizens. Rather, he felt that social science, properly used and understood, had liberating possibilities. Just as knowledge of the laws of aerodynamics enabled flight and greater freedom to travel, Dewey believed that a fuller understanding of individual and social behavior would free individuals and their communities from the restrictions often imposed by outdated traditions.

This did not mean that he promoted a blanket condemnation of traditional forms of life. However, it did suggest that sometimes traditions become dysfunctional, especially as the natural and social environment change. It also suggests that when they become dysfunctional the social science can serve to open up new and more productive connections—new avenues of engagement, new experiential possibilities. Dewey expected that the social sciences more fully developed could provoke more intelligent, participatory, democratic control.

Dewey's Moral Theory

The idea of a tradition grown dysfunctional opens up two additional features of Dewey's system: his moral theory and his understanding of individual and social behavior.

In contrast to classical liberal theory that depicted people as inherently passive needing to be goaded into action by either rewards or punishment, Dewey believed people to be essentially interested and active. If they were passive, it was because they had *learned* to be submissive—a trait that Dewey held was antithetical to democracy. As Murray G. Murphey reported in his introduction to Dewey's *Human Nature and Conduct*, "Nothing so aroused Dewey's scorn as the psychological dogma that humans are naturally passive and must be compelled to act."[18] And, "The task of childrearing is to coordinate *innate energy* into effective action."[19]

For Dewey, effective action entails coordinating behavior toward a given end-in-view. The idea of end-in-view indicates both the inherent connection between means and ends and also that ends and means undergo change as they interact with environmental constraints. Much of this coordination is automatic. For example, when a person is learning to drive a car, he is consciously aware of each step in the process: how far to turn the steering wheel, how much pressure to place on the gas pedal or the brake, exactly where to focus the eyes. In contrast, the *seasoned* driver executes all of these automatically and can focus on other tasks. What is the speed limit? Where should I turn? Where is the nearest gas station? What will I say at my meeting?

Habit involves the successful coordination of complex functional behaviors for the purpose of reaching given goals. It is manifested in response to certain environmental situation that we can perform usually without conscious attention. At times, too much thinking can become problematic. The slumping baseball player who tries to recall exactly how far he spread his feet the last time he hit a ball is unlikely to hit the ball. Yet there are also times when thinking is exactly what is needed as when a situation has become unsettled. Thinking about action involves breaking a task into smaller units, end-in-view, or a goal, along with the plan to achieve it. When we evaluate an act for Dewey, we must also consider the likelihood and the worth of the means to achieve it.

There is a social side to individual habit that is reflected in various kinds of conventions, laws, customs and traditions. These often arise out of some kind of necessity, but the ways this necessity is collectively resolved may be somewhat arbitrary from a historical standpoint. We must be able to predict how other drivers on the road will behave and so we agree to certain, otherwise arbitrary rules. Red (not purple) means stop; green (not tan) means go. Drive on the right side, pass on the left and so forth. These rules may or may not be written down, and they may or may not be enforced by law, but they at the very least carry the weight of convention or custom.

Custom is to the society what habit is to the individual. It is a conventional way of coordinating expectations so that activity can proceed smoothly without conflict or interruption. Many customs exist prior to the birth of any one individual and are formed and perpetuated by individuals as participants of a group. They are formulas of behavior that serve to guide individual habit—do it this way not that. In Japan, it is *expected that the host will* provide the guest with a pleasant cup of tea without asking. In the United States, one ask the guest whether she would like a soft drink or a hard, tea or coffee, black or with cream etc.[20]

Of course, even people brought up in the same group with the same customs will not all share the same traits—some may be more adventuresome than others, some may be more honest etc. The difference is sometimes described as character. However, to belong to the same group means that there is a shared, direct intelligibility to moral action. Even though you are more courageous than I am, I understand what courage means in much the same way that you do. And this shared understanding provides meaning to everyday life. Because we share these meanings we know who our heroes are. We know what is expected of us as we fill our everyday roles and go on with our everyday lives.[21]

Shared meanings make individual habits and moral behavior intelligible to people. One of the reasons some people are uncomfortable with the idea of multi-culturalism is because they are afraid that once-shared meanings and behaviors will no longer be collectively intelligible. For example, when I was maybe ten years old, I was ambling down the street when an older woman, coming in the opposite direction, unintentionally blocked my way, as I, unintentionally, blocked hers. She went to her right. I went to my left. She went to her left, I to my right. At that point, she became visibly annoyed and informed me of "a rule" that I was *supposed* to stop to let her pass by. I had not heard of this rule and felt quite embarrassed that I did not know it. Yet I am still not sure whether any such rule existed, other than "in her head" (excuse me, Dewey). And if it did, I am still not sure why it was my responsibility to stop. Was it because I was younger and she older? Or was it because I was a male and she female? Or perhaps it was because I was walking north and she south? Yet, if there had been such a rule it, had it been known and followed, it certainly would have avoided confusion and misstep. Habit and custom are conventions that are not formalized into law but allow for coordinated behavior and enable things to get done. For Dewey, they form much of the basis for that other-serving behavior, which is part of what it means to be moral. However, Dewey notes that when these customs and habits become inflexible; they are subject to decay and disintegration, and morality then calls for reflection and change. The problem is also that when conditions change, existing customs may no longer function as expected. That is why rigidity is a problem in certain kinds of situations. It does not allow for needed change.

Dewey on Moral Education

Moral education for Dewey involves the development of the capacity to reflect on existing habits and customs, recognizing those that have become dysfunctional. It also involves the capacity to project and to experiment with alternatives courses of action that could further additional growth.

For Dewey, every pedagogical act potentially communicates a moral message, but not every pedagogical act is teaching students to be moral in the sense of the development of the kind of reflective experimental spirit that moral behavior in the modern age requires. One of Dewey's deep educational concerns was the possibility of moral *miseducation*. This occurs not only, or not even primarily, as the result of direct instruction as much as it does through the very organization of the school day. Requiring students to sit in rows with hands on their desk, to compete with one another for recognition and to repeat, parrot-like, some moral catechism is to deliver the wrong moral message—be quiet and follow orders! It is wrong because it is antithetical to reflection, experimentation and thought, qualities that he considered critical for democracy.

For Dewey, effective moral thinking involves "the complete act of thought" and is no different in kind from other kinds of good thinking. In *How We Think*, Dewey famously summarized the process as involving five steps.

> (i) a felt difficulty; (ii) its location and definition; (iii) suggestion of possible solution; (iv) development by reasoning of the bearings of the suggestion; (v) further observation and experiment leading to its acceptance or rejection; that is, the conclusion of belief or disbelief.[22]

The process applies equally whether the difficulty arises because a mechanic needs to fix the engine of a car, or because a teacher needs to address the effects of a classroom bully. Morality as well as mechanics requires reflective intelligent thought. And, of course, mechanics and other seemingly technical practices have potential moral consequences as, for example, with an inadequate break repair.

As Dewey puts it: "Moral growth . . . may be described as a process in which man (sic) becomes more *rational*, more *social*, and finally more *moral*."[23]

The Twofold Meaning of Moral Development

Moral development meant two things for Dewey. First, it meant the development of a child's capacity to understand, evaluate and intelligently contribute to a community. Second, it meant the development of a moral community itself so that its members can intelligently assess and change habits and customs in order to adequately respond to changing conditions. He believed both forms of development were critical tasks for education but were not confined to one subject. Instead, moral education was a task for the entire community. The moral task of the school is to assure that the student develops the habits of reflection, intelligence and experimentation—the habits of inquiry and cooperation. Moral education involves refining the interaction between a child and her social and physical environment in ways that encourages careful cooperation and inquiry. One of the aims of moral education is to enable students to reflect on otherwise routine habits and customs in order to find ways to address problematic situations.

Custom, like habit, is simply the crystallization of past acts of successful valuation, that new and changing conditions can render dysfunctional. The one, habit, is an attribute of individuals. The other, custom is an attribute of social groups. Both are formed under specific conditions and when conditions change these both may need to be reevaluated, modified or changed. This process involves reflection and is a critical feature of any education.

Was Dewey a Moral Relativist?

Dewey is often criticized for being a moral relativist. This criticism is meant to indicate two things. First, it suggests that Dewey has no moral principles, and, second, it implies that

Dewey believes that morality is a subjective matter only. Both of these interpretations are inaccurate. Again, the Civil War can provide and instructive example. The problem of the Civil War was not that one camp had principle on its side and the other was without principle. The problem was that both sides appealed passionately to conflicting principles. To oversimplify, one side appealed to individual freedom; the other side appealed to the right of states to determine their own policies. One side saw *United States* of America as a plurality. The other envisaged it as a single country. The dispute was most importantly over slavery, but it was also over the grammatical status of the term "United States of America"—plural or singular noun.

Dewey believed that intractable moral conflicts arise when parties appeal dogmatically to conflicting principles without proposing any means to test them. Nevertheless, he held that moral claims, like any claims, are objective in the sense that they can be tested against experience. For example, if a person argues for capital punishment because she believes that it deters crime, this belief can be tested in terms of whether there is less or more crime. Of course, there are other justifications for capital punishment and other reasons to oppose it, but it would certainly weaken the case for the practice if the empirical claims were shown not to hold up.

Still, the view that moral claims are objective is one of the more controversial of Dewey's ideas. Many philosophers, including me, contend that Dewey commits what they term "the naturalistic fallacy." The naturalistic fallacy holds that logically you cannot conclude that something *ought* to be the case from the fact that something *is* the case.

Yet Dewey would likely respond that the idea that going from *is* to *ought* or from fact to value is thought to be a fallacy is problematic in its own right. It suggests that moral knowledge is somehow special and that certainty is the goal of moral inquiry. Sometimes, this "special knowledge" is thought of as *moral* intuition. Kant called this moral apperception, or a judgment that is grounded outside of conscious thought. Examples would be a parent's uncalculated response to a baby's cry or the revulsion someone feels about an execution of an innocent person or a child's unnecessary suffering. John Rawls, for example, held that moral reasoning about justice requires that we adopt the standpoint of fictive choosers who, having no idea what class or group they belong to, must select rules of social justice.[24] Other philosophers, such as Kant, think of moral reasoning as the recognition of others as human beings and hence as subject to special consideration—treat others as an end and not as a means only. Many religious thinkers believe that the Bible provides a definitive code for moral action.

Dewey takes a different tack. He brings moral deliberation down to earth and makes it less special. It is part of our everyday life. For him, morality means "growth of conduct in meaning ... It means that kind of expansion in meaning which is consequent upon observations of the conditions and outcome of conduct."[25] The more I am aware of both the direct and indirect consequences of my action, the more intelligent, effective and moral is my future action likely to be. Dewey's focus is not only on the act itself but on the evaluative process as well and specifically on the connection between the consequences and the means to achieve them—i.e. the ends-in-view discussed previously.

No End Without Means

There is a confusion here that I think can be cleared up. Dewey and his interlockers are discussing different things. His critics are focusing on the question of moral knowledge and what it is. Dewey is focusing on thinking, including thinking about moral questions, and how to improve it. For Dewey, there is never an end that is just a good in-itself. Its goodness can only be evaluated in conjunction with an evaluation of the means required to achieve it, and its consequences for other goods. Are the means effective? Are they efficient? Is the end worth the cost? How can I balance conflicting goods? Education provides all kinds of examples where the means and the end intertwine. Suppose, for example, that you develop a method for teaching reading that is effective in getting children to read but is so distasteful that they never want to pick up a book. Shaming poor readers would be another extreme example. Assume that it is more effective than any other method—a big assumption—any measure of its worth would need to include its possible side-effects in say a sense of self-doubt, insecurity or servility. In other words, Dewey's view of the process of moral decision-making is on the same plane as his view of the process of decision-making as a whole, and decision-making as a whole always has a potentially moral quality to it.

Moral Evolution

A key to understanding Dewey's view of morality is to place custom and habit discussed earlier in a historical, evolutionary perspective where situations change and, as a result, what counts as a functional response needs to change as well. A tradition or custom that is appropriate or functional for one kind of situation is not so for another.

Consider the changes that have occurred in the way women have come to be addressed during my lifetime. When I was younger, it was considered polite to address a woman as either Miss or Mrs. (followed by her husband's last name). A mistake—call a Mrs. a Miss or call a Miss a Mrs.—could be taken as offensive. Over time, Ms. became the preferred title, especially but not exclusively in professional settings. Now, to call professional women "Miss." or "Mrs." and not "Ms." in certain settings can be considered deeply offensive. The same kind of change in behavior happens in terms of non-verbal protocols. When I was a young man it was expected that I would open a door for a woman in almost any situation. Again, over time, this protocol changed, and opening the door sometimes became a matter for subtle negotiation—is it polite or patronizing? This may seem like a small matter, but it involves deep moral issues about equality. One reason for this shift has been a change in the work situation of women and in the fact that marriage is now only one possible path for women to aspire to. In addition, women may not want to be treated as helpless beings that need a strong man to open the door. Most feel more than capable to open the door for themselves—thank you! Dewey might trace the change back to a critical technological revolution like the capacity of a woman to control the timing of childbirth and the possibilities it created.

The example points to some critical aspects of Dewey's moral theory. First, the simplest act can become a focus of moral concern. Second, the moral quality of an act is tied to a wider system of meaning. Third, the evaluation of moral action will involve an evaluation of that system of meaning in terms of the consequences of the behavior. Fourth, the evaluation will take place in terms of human growth and the quality of human experience. To return to the earlier example, the reason why Mrs. *Husbands name* is objectionable to some people in some situations is not just that it is inappropriate, but, more importantly, because it has implications for the growth and development of an entire group of people based on factors that have nothing to do with talent or ability. Now I would argue that there is a fairly basic moral principle here that has to do with the deep belief that to judge and treat a person on the basis of accidental qualities that they cannot control is wrong unless there is some overwhelming task related reason for doing so. Inquiry is a critical factor in moral deliberation simply because technology often makes something that counts as an overriding reason for one generation irrelevant one for another.

This point is exactly what the attacks on "political correctness" fail to acknowledge. Conditions change and as they do there is a need to reflect on existing habits, customs and laws. To introduce a high-powered professional woman today as Mrs. (husband's name) involves more than a simple mistake. It is to label her in terms of someone else's status. It is an attack on meanings that liberate women from a narrow range of opportunities.

Responsibility

For Dewey, moral education is education for social awareness and for social inquiry, and it involves the development of a sense of responsibility, which arises first because others hold us accountable for our act. A child spills milk and is expected to clean it up. Giving reasons may or may not play a role here depending on many factors. Cultural factors may influence the way disapproval is expressed, but disapproval is certainly not just an inner state of mind.

> Approbation and disapprobation are ways of influencing the formation of habits and aims; that is, of influencing future acts. The

individual is *held* accountable for what he *has* done in order that he may be responsive in what he is *going* to do. Gradually persons learn by dramatic imitation to hold themselves accountable, and liability becomes a voluntary deliberate acknowledgment that deeds are our own, that their consequences come from us.[26]

Dewey is not suggesting that everything that is social is moral and everything that is individual is evil. As he continues:

There is no excuse for thinking of evil action as individualistic and right action as social. Deliberate unscrupulous pursuit of self-interest is as much conditioned upon social opportunities, training and assistance as is the course of action prompted by a beaming benevolence. The difference lies in the quality and degree of the perception of ties and interdependencies; in the use to which they are put . . . A man may attempt to utilize social relationships for his own advantage in an inequitable way; he may intentionally or unconsciously try to make them feed one of his own appetites. Then he is denounced as egoistic. But both his course of action and the disapproval he is subject to are facts *within* society. They are social phenomena. He pursues his unjust advantage as a social asset[27]

One answer to the question of whether Dewey is a moral relativist is a qualified yes, but only in so far as moral intelligibility contributes to the stability of a society and allows its members to grow. So, by evaluating a piece of social behavior, we can determine just what social function it serves, and why. Was it once useful, and, if so, then does it still serve that or some other justifiable purpose? These questions provide a rational for Dewey's typical method of seeking the origins of a habit in order to determine its appropriateness for the present situation.

Critical Questions

So a contrarian philosopher might ask: Does this answer mean that Dewey would accept slavery if it were part of a well-ordered, stable society or that he would accept the subjugation of women where sexual equality would create confusion or uncertainty? These questions are certainly not of the same order as whether eating lamb or not eating lamb is a sign of a morally advanced society. Given Dewey's treatment of morality the answer to these questions from his standpoint may be more nuanced than some, including myself, will be comfortable with. Certainly, an absolute prohibition on slavery or paternalism would seem called for today, and any equivocation would be more than wrong. It would be abetting evil. Dewey proposed an evolutionary explanation:

> Even if the words remain the same they mean something very different when they are uttered by a minority struggling against repressive measures and when a group that, having attained power, then use ideas that were once weapons of emancipation as instruments for keeping the power and wealth it has obtained. Ideas that at one time are means of producing social change assume another guise when they are used as a means of preventing further social change.[28]

The passage is consistent with Dewey's larger understanding of co-evolution, which he advances in the opening pages of his *Logic*:

> Upon the biological level, organisms have to respond to conditions about them in ways that modify those conditions and the relations of organisms to them so as to restore the reciprocal adaptation that is required for the maintenance of life-functions. Human organisms are involved in the same sort of predicament. Because of the effect

> of cultural conditions, the problems involved not only have different contents but are capable of statement *as* problems so that inquiry can enter as a factor in their resolution.[29]

There is a great deal to be said for Dewey's evolutionary view of ethics. Our ideas about good and bad do change over time in response to changing events and conditions. Yet the example of slavery and the Civil War challenges the other side of this evolutionary ethics. Was slavery itself ever a justifiable response to cultural conditions? I think not, and I do not believe that Dewey would believe this either. Nevertheless, Dewey's evolutionary formulation lures us to overthink the matter. Yes, as some have argued, perhaps slavery might have ended on its own accord, but this in itself does not mitigate the evil that was slavery. James, atypically, may have had a more satisfying response when he argues seemingly in contradiction to his subjective view of truth, for an understanding of morals as objective and universal. "Were there left but one rock with two loving souls upon it, that rock would have as thoroughly a moral constitution as any possible world."[30]

For Dewey, the changes wrought by industrialization required that the process of coevolution be undertaken consciously and collectively, and he believed that public schools held out the promise for consciously directing it in a meaningful way. He summarized this belief in the concluding sentences of his 1897 short classic, *My Pedagogical Creed*:

> I believe that when science and art thus join hands the most commanding motive for human action will be reached; the most genuine springs of human conduct aroused and the best service that human nature is capable of guaranteed.

> I believe, finally, that the teacher is engaged, not simply in the training of individuals, but in the formation of the proper social life.
>
> I believe that every teacher should realize the dignity of his calling; that he is a social servant set apart for the maintenance of proper social order and the securing of the right social growth.
>
> I believe that in this way the teacher always is the prophet of the true God and the usher in of the true kingdom of God.[31]

Dewey's title for the heading of this evangelical-like passage, "The School and Social Progress," is also an apt label for the social imaginary that propelled Dewey's educational writings. That such rhetoric, if written today, would seem way over the top suggests just how much that social imaginary has changed since Dewey began writing about education.

Notes

1. Past Masters, *The Collected Works of John Dewey 1882–1953*, Past Masters, http://pm.nlx.com.proxy2.library.illinois.edu/xtf/view?docId=dewey/dewey.32.xml;chunk.id=div.lw.12.12;toc.id=div.lw.12.8;brand=default
2. Philip W. Jackson, *John Dewey and the Lessons of Art* (New Haven: Yale University Press, 1998), p. 11.
3. John Dewey, *Experience and Nature* (New York: Dover, 1925/1959), p. 303.
4. John Dewey, *How We Think* (Buffalo, NY: Prometheus Books, 1991), p. 125.
5. Ibid., p. 122.
6. Ibid., p. 130.
7. John Dewey, *Art as Experience* (New York: Perigee Books, 1934/1980), p. 35.
8. Dewey, *Experience and Nature*, p. 177.
9. John Dewey, "The Reflex Arc Concept in Psychology," *Psychological Review*, 3 (1896), pp. 357–370.
10. John Dewey, *Theory of Evaluation: International Encyclopedia of Unified Science*, Vol. 2 (Chicago: University of Chicago Press, 1939), p. 9.
11. Dewey, *Experience and Nature*, p. 167.

12. Ibid., p. 173.
13. Ibid., p. 235.
14. Ibid., p. 237.
15. Michael C. Corballis, *The Truth about Language: What It Is and Where It Came From* (Chicago: University of Chicago Press, 2017), pp. 44–45.
16. Thomas M. Alexander, *John Dewey's Theory of Art, Experience & Nature: The Horizons of Feeling* (New York: SUNY Press, 1987), p. XVIII.
17. John Dewey, *Democracy and Education* (New York: The Free Press, 1916), p. 29.
18. Murray G. Murphey, "Introduction," John Dewey, *Human Nature and Conduct 1922* (Carbondale: Southern Illinois University Press, 1922/1988), p. X.
19. Ibid.
20. Takeo Doi, *Anatomy of Dependence* (Tokyo: Kodansha International, 1971), p. 11.
21. Walter Feinberg, *What Is a Public Education and Why We Need It: A Philosophical Inquiry into Self-Development, Cultural Commitment, and Public Engagement* (Lanham: Lexington Books, 2016), Chapter 2.
22. Dewey, *How We Think, The Middle Works*, V. 5, p. 237.
23. *The Middle Works of John Dewey, 1899–1924*, Vol. 5, p. 16. My "sic" to qualify Dewey's "man" is itself a product of historical reflection on established custom.
24. John Rawls, *A Theory of Justice* (Cambridge: Harvard University Press, 1974).
25. Dewey, *Human Nature and Conduct*, p. 194.
26. *Human Nature and Conduct in Collected Works*, Middle Works 1894–1924, Vol. 14 (Carbondale: Southern Illinois University Press, 2003), p. 218.
27. Ibid.
28. John Dewey, *Liberalism and Social Action* in Collected Works 1925–1953, Vol. 11 (Carbondale: Southern Illinois University Press, 2003), p. 292.
29. John Dewey, *Logic*.
30. William James, "The Moral Philosopher and the Moral Life," in Bruce Wilshire (ed.) William James, *The Essential Writings* (New York: Harper and Row, 1971), p. 303.
31. John Dewey, "My Pedagogical Creed," *School Journal*, 54 (January 1897), p. 80.

4

DEWEY ON EDUCATION

Introduction: Education as Communal Continuity and Renewal: A Civil War Legacy

For Dewey, education, whether it occurs in a formal school or elsewhere, is the process by which immature individuals learn to participate in the meanings of their community and through which communities renew themselves across generations. At the time Dewey began thinking about education the Civil War had disrupted the local sectional communities, and the United States was in the early stages of national re*generation*; compulsory education laws were being enacted across the country, until finally, in 1917, Mississippi completed the process begun by Massachusetts in 1852. Whether he realized it or not, Dewey's definition of education as the source of social renewal and continuity was more than a philosophical abstraction. It defined the national project to enact the Constitution's vision of "a more perfect union." For Dewey that vision required a new set of possibilities, rooted not in sectional antagonisms, but in the new possibilities that science and democracy allowed. With some exceptions of course, his faith in the unifying, democratic mission of public education would reiterate the optimism and trust that much of the population would place in the public schools.

For Dewey, education involves those practices whereby children come to share in the inherited skills, understandings and values of the community as they take on its aims as their aims, identify its history as their history and come to care about its well-being as they would care about their own, individual well-being. Yet democratic education is more than just community reproduction where one generation takes on the customs, traditions and skills of the previous generation. A democratic education is also community renewal and reconstruction. "What the best and wisest parent wants for his own child, that must the community want for all of its children." And what a democratic community must want for its children is greater opportunity and growth. Because education is the process by which a community renews itself, it is also the concern of everyone in that community. Dewey's vision of a national democratic community concerned about its own renewal through the education of all its children has never been fully realized, but it did capture the imagination of many citizens, new and old alike, well after the memory of the War between the North and the South had faded from the forefront of the national consciousness and had been replaced by a new concern—defining and constructing a country of immigrants.

Education v. Schooling

As mentioned previously, Dewey distinguished between *education* as the intergenerational renewal of social life and *schooling* as the specialized formal institution of intentional instruction. Formal schooling regulates transmission for the purpose of communal continuity. The school, Dewey tells us, "is simply that form of community life in which all those agencies are concentrated that will be most effective in bringing the child to share in the inherited resources of the race, and to use his own powers for social ends."[1]

The definition is revealing for a few reasons. First, it is an aspirational definition. It serves not to mark off what is but rather what should be. Not everything we call a "school" will fit his idea of a school, but all schools should strive to do so. Second, he likely has in mind a certain kind of community, namely a democratic community, as he conceived it. Third, this definition highlights the communal aspect of the school and implicitly deemphasizes a more traditional concept of school as a place where teachers *transmit* some specific subject to students. In highlighting the communal role of the school, Dewey is not rejecting its more traditional definition as a place where teachers teach a subject and students learn it. Rather, he is highlighting a broader aspect of the school's role as an educational agency—its role in reproducing a society—and a different conception of learning, one where active participation is a critical factor. This idea of active participation gives agency to the students as well as the community, and it is critical in distinguishing schooling as a mere socializing institution that stamps a pre-established identity on children and a communal one that recognizes the importance of agency as a process of co-defining one's identity with that of a community.

But now, one might ask: Why does Dewey highlight these features, making them critical for schooling? After all, would not it be more fitting and efficient to allow a family and its selected community to socialize children, while giving the schools the more specialized task of teaching children basic skills, such as basic literacy and numeracy? This idea of a strong division of labor between home and school is the basis of many conservative proposals to restrict schools to the teaching of "essential" skills while leaving to the home and the church the task of teaching values. It is also an argument for streamlining the schools and eliminating so called "frill subjects." The answer to this question requires that we look at the social conditions at the time Dewey began to write about schools, and it requires us to examine how he thought about the idea of an "essential" skill.

Dewey in the Context of His Time

It is well to recall that at the time Dewey began to write about education in the late 1800s, compulsory schooling was not yet the law in a number of states, and yet, the Civil War had planted the idea of a larger national identity. Dewey understood that something more was at stake than just developing basic skills. He opined that in times past when schools had been a minor part of children's lives, it mattered little that the curriculum was narrow and shallow. Socialization was then a side effect of growing up in a community. Children performed jobs at home and there they learned the discipline of work. They cared for farm animals, and through that caring, they learned about sexual reproduction. They worked the fields in the spring and enjoyed the harvest in the fall and in the process learned certain critical values like the benefits of patience and deferring gratification. They participated in community events and learned the importance of charity by close contact with the needy. In other words, socialization was largely the task of the community. There children could learn most of all they needed about life. And because the community did so much, the schools of the past could do much less. By the late 1800s, this was changing. Trends that had begun prior to the Civil War, such as the spread and intensification of factory work, were drastically accelerated after the War ended, and this set the stage for Dewey's ideas about educational innovation.

As Dewey began to write about education, the real world of life and work was changing from home-based production and relative self-sufficiency of rural life to factory-based production and the interdependence of industrial production and urban life. Dewey opined that as a result much that once had been learned informally through family and farm life had to be intentionally taught in formal schools. He believed that as the rural, farming community became a smaller part of a child's life, the school needed to become a larger part. He also believed that the school could serve to reintroduce children to their community at the same time that it extended their outlook beyond it. In the absence of transformative progressive schools, he held that urban life and industrialization threatened the child's meaningful incorporation into a democratic community, and he feared that traditional schools would fail to develop in children the basic values required by a democratic way of life.

Dewey feared too that without an educational transformation, children would not develop a meaningful connection to a larger community, and that subject matter taught just for its own sake without regard to their real-life function would be too abstract to be meaningful. He likened this dystopian possibility to trying to teach a person how to swim without ever going near the water, requiring them to practice their stroke while lying on the sand. When this happens, both life and learning lose their meaning. Dewey hoped that a reformed system of schooling could connect subject matter to the child's active interests and to those of a wider, more democratic community. He believed that because the industrial setting separated the child from the ongoing life of the community the time was ripe for a new progressive approach to schooling. As he wrote:

> No training of sense-organs in schools, introduced for the sake of training, can begin to compete with the alertness and fullness of sense-life that comes through daily intimacy and interest in familiar occupations. Verbal memory can be trained in committing tasks, a certain discipline of reasoning powers can be acquired through lessons in science and mathematics; but, after all, this is somewhat remote and shadowy compared with the training of attention and of judgment that is acquired in having to do things with a real motive and real outcomes ahead. At present, concentration of industry and division of labor have practically eliminated household and neighborhood occupations—at least for educational purposes.[2]

The Real World of Public Schools

In a muckraking series on schools published in the early 1890s, J. M. Rice captured something of the disquieting dark features of traditional schools. He depicted the public school as being comprised of autocratic teachers, subservient students and mindless lessons. In his shocking expose, Rice surveyed schools in a number of American cities such as New York, Chicago, St. Paul and Boston during 1892–1893, finding in all shallow, mind-deadening practices. Here is his report of a reading lesson in Chicago:

> When some time had been spent in thus maneuvering the jaw, the teacher remarked: "your tongues are not loose." Fifty pupils now put out their tongues and wagged them in all directions. What an idea these pupils must have received of the purpose of a school when from the start they were taught systematically how to make grimaces and wag their tongues! . . .
>
> In another classroom the pupils threw their glances around in a horrible manner when reading; they stared frightfully. I mentioned this to the principal who informed me in reply that this room was noted for the manner in which pupils used their eyes and that it was, in consequence generally known as "the eye room."[3]

Rice went on to described a school in New York that had been rated as excellent by the New York School Superintendent as

> [t]he most dehumanizing institution that I have ever laid eyes upon, each child being treated as if he possessed a memory and the faculty of speech but no individuality, no sensibility, no soul . . . The spirit of the school is, "do what you like with the child, immobilize him, automize him, dehumanize him, but save, save the minutes." Everything is prohibited that is of no measurable advantage to the child, such as movement of the head or limb, when there is no logical reason why it should be moved at that time. I asked the principle whether the children were not allowed to move their heads. "Why should they look behind when the teacher is in front of them?": words too logical to be refuted.[4]

Perhaps the key sentence here for Dewey would have been, "Why should they look behind when the teacher is in front of them?" For Dewey, the children in these schools are being taught to obey an arbitrary authority and blindly to follow its orders, the antithesis of the needs of a democratic society and of a democratic way of life.

For Dewey, schools like those Rice described were little more than training grounds for future alienated adults who would be able to endure a world without meaning. In his chapter entitled "Experience and Thinking" in his classic book *Democracy and Education*, Dewey might have had Rice's series in mind when he wrote: "The nervous strain and fatigue which results with both teacher and pupil are a necessary consequence of the abnormality of the situation in which bodily activity is divorced from the perception of meaning."[5]

Learning by Doing

From 1894 to 1904, Dewey served as Head of the new Laboratory School at the University of Chicago, and he also headed the Department of Philosophy, Psychology and Pedagogy at the same university. A goal of his laboratory school was to provide a new, activity-based model for education. In contrast to children in more traditional classrooms where students were expected to sit silently except when they were called on to recite, the students in Dewey's school moved around and were engaged in cooperative activity and hands on projects. Because children were encouraged to be active and engaged, teachers did not have to order them to sit down or to be quiet. Activity, talk and collaboration were important parts of education. Here the authority of the project was paramount rather than the authority of the biggest person in the room—the teacher.

And the children themselves were to have a say in how the task would be accomplished. Dewey also believed that by engaging the active interest of the child, the traditional subjects could be taught in a more meaningful and effective way.

Progressive education was known for the slogan "learning by doing," but the full meaning of this slogan is not self-evident. Some educators have interpreted it to mean that every subject must be taught for its practical, hands on implications. So, for example, physics might be taught in terms or the laws governing the riding of a bike or the physics of hitting a home run. While these are possibly productive methods for teaching physics in some cases, Dewey means something considerably broader than this. He means that much learning often occurs by indirection through the act of doing something. As he notes,

> Children do not set out, consciously, to learn walking or talking. One sets out to give his impulse for communication and fuller intercourse with others a show . . . The better methods of teaching a child to read . . . do not fix his attention upon the fact that he has to learn something . . . They engage his activities, then in the process of engagement he learns.[6]

While Dewey often made the point that education was not preparation for some distant future, he did not mean that education should be indifferent to the capacity of the child to function later in life. He meant that preparation for life must not defer meaning to some future time. It must begin by taking into account the experiences and the interests that children bring to the school from their life outside and then to use those experiences to stimulate the child and then to extend that interest beyond the familiar. In truth, this *is* preparation. It is modeling life in a democratic community where experience is meaningful and where citizens are agents of their individual and collective destinies.

Learning by doing also suggested that learning is initiated by a problematic situation. The child does not learn to walk by consciously deciding: "I want to walk." The child has a goal in mind, for example, reaching for a toy or a person, an outstretched arm and then, often with the initial coaxing of others, takes a first step. No one tells him to put the right foot in front of the left and then the left in from of the right. Rather by aiming towards a goal—grasping the arm or the ball—the child takes a tentative step towards the goal, falls, gets up takes two more steps, and then eventually not only reaches the goal but begins to enjoy her new mode of mobility. There is a certain wonder to the whole thing from both the adult's and the child's standpoint. Look at what she did! Look at me—hey, I'm moving!

A problematic situation is the beginning of thought, and the successful act is its completion. In between there are all kinds of trials and errors. When we take note of these, make them conscious, keep track of them, try to understand why some work and why some don't and begin to consciously experiment with different methods, then we are thinking.

As we have seen, for Dewey, children are naturally active, and this activity is already directed, through interest, toward some aim. The task for education then is to harness this interest and engage the child's natural activity in ways that will broaden and deepen experience. The *what* of learning—subject matter—is tied to the *how* of learning—pedagogy—in terms of the shaping of students' character and their relationship to their community. For example, students who are taught history or arithmetic in rote and mechanical ways, as one meaningless fact after another, will likely come to learn the lesson that history and arithmetic are fixed meaningless facts with little relevance to ongoing concerns. Students who are encouraged to see arithmetic as a part of their everyday world and history at work in their local community will likely experience the significance of these subjects for understanding broader areas of life and learn to use them to address individual and community concerns.

The connection between the subject matter and the method of education is a critical aspect of Dewey's educational philosophy and reflects his understanding of mind that I addressed in the last chapter. For Dewey, if the active nature of the child is to be preserved and her experience deepened, then the subject matter must connect in some organic way to the child's ongoing life experience. Again, this does not mean, as both some followers and some critics of Dewey have assumed, that these subjects must always be tethered to some narrow practical form of life. It simply means that the natural progression of children, including their immediate interests, and needs must be taken into account as they expand both their interests and their skills.

The teacher's ultimate concern is the growth of the child through the deepening of experience. One danger of strictly formal instruction is that it can kill motivation by ignoring the interest of the child or by corralling her inherently active nature, making her a passive receptor of the information provided by someone else. For Dewey, the teacher's task should be to provide an organic connection between the child's past and present experience through the subject matter. In his laboratory school at the University of Chicago, activities like weaving, cooking, manual training, drawing etc. were used to highlight the connection between the present and the past and between learning and doing and to engage students collaboratively to experiment with different ways to solve problems.

Although his curriculum included practical activities like sewing and weaving and gardening, its purpose was not narrow vocational training. Dewey understood that these practices were fast becoming obsolete as common modes of production. Rather, these activities had social as well as immediate pedagogical value. As he wrote:

> We are apt to look at the school from an individualistic standpoint, as something between teacher and pupil, or between teacher and parent. That which interests us most is naturally the progress made by the individual child of our acquaintance, his normal physical development, his advance in ability to read, write, and figure, his growth in the knowledge of geography and history, improvement in manners, habits of promptness, order, and industry—it is from such standards as these that we judge the work of the school. And rightly so. Yet the range of the outlook needs to be enlarged . . . All that society has accomplished for itself is put, through the agency of the school, at the disposal of its future members. All its better thoughts of itself it hopes to realize through the new possibilities thus opened to its future self. Here individualism and socialism are at one.[7]

The school in Dewey's view should serve as an instrument of progressive social change by providing children with an idealized view of social progress and future possibilities.

For the most part, the darker side of "progress" was filtered out of the Deweyian school, and little efforts was made to incorporate the voices of oppressed groups, African Americans, Native Americans, etc. Today, as we will see in the last chapter, the appropriateness of this filter divides contemporary educators, even many influenced by Dewey. Some hold that schools should not minimize the oppressive tendencies of society, but rather should present them in an accurate way. Others believe that healthy development requires a strong filter and that children should be presented with an idealized version of the past and its future possibilities. By default, Dewey embraced this latter view, perhaps without realizing that from the standpoint of oppressed groups, it presented a distorted view of history and an overly idealized view of America's past. This is why today, some people complain that they do not recognize themselves in the way the story of America is told. In promoting the community he wanted, Dewey neglected the community that was and that had been.

The Logic of the Expert

In *My Pedagogical Creed*, Dewey defined educational method as the law for presenting and treating material and he held that this law requires that education follow the development of the child's own powers and interest.[8] This definition is often misunderstood and interpreted to mean that method is more important than subject matter. This misunderstanding is one of the reasons Dewey is often lumped uncritically with child-centered educators and criticized for minimizing the importance of subject matter. In his book *Democracy and Education*, Dewey provides a more detailed account of his view tying both method and subject matter to the unity of the thought process. Method is simply an orderly means to accomplish an end. It is part of a practice, and every efficient activity must have a method. Content or subject matter is what one attends to in acting efficiently to solve problems.

The film *Hidden Figures* provides a striking example of Dewey's point. The film, based on real people and events, is about a group of brilliant African American women who worked as calculators for NASA in the early days of the space program. At the time, the NASA facility was segregated, and very few women, let alone African American women, worked at anything other than menial positions in the program. The dramatic moment in the film comes when the scientists are trying to figure the exact landing spot of John Glenn's space craft—the first American manned flight to circle the globe. The problem turns out to be too complex for traditional, tried-and-true math methods to handle, and all of the calculations are dangerously off base. In the film, Katherine Goble Johnson, an African American woman and math virtuoso, suggests that they use an older method, the Euler method, to address the problem. It works, and the flight ends safely. In this case, the task was to get Glenn home safely. In this episode, a more flexible understanding of math was critical.

Yet, in actual fact, math was but one of many specialties employed in the work of the Center. Human relations and applied sociology would have been critical in selecting and developing teams. Of course math would have been critical in a number of other ways as well such as design and construction, budget analysis, etc. The problem of building, flying and landing a spacecraft was a multidisciplinary affair where synchronization across fields of knowledge was critical. In the scene portrayed in the film, expert knowledge is more than just knowing a subject, and it is more than just being able to employ a certain method—over time, the human calculators were replaced by computers.

Expert knowledge also involves something about the way the knowledge is held. In *Hidden Figures*, it involved a capacity to reflect upon the standard tried-and-true method of calculating orbit trajectories and realizing that a different method is more suitable to the problem at hand. The episode suggests that expert knowledge is not just knowing *that* something is the case or knowing *how* to perform a task. Expert knowledge involves a capacity to reflect on existing methods and subject matter. The film also highlights the importance of the capacity to listen to and hear different points of view, something that is missing in the ideal of expertise when narrowly construed.

Implications for Teaching

For Dewey, two standpoints are important for teachers. There is the standpoint of the expert, the person who already has mastered the activity, and there is the standpoint of the learner, or the novice. The teacher's task is to build a bridge between the two. The bridge is built while engaging the child's active interest and present skills. We learn to walk by walking, not by consciously setting out to walk.[9] The same should be true of other activities. Children learn to talk because of a natural desire to communicate with others. It is a part of their identity as a social self. The same can be said for reading or writing; these are extensions of the child's natural desire to communicate by participating in a narrative. To teach children to read, it is useful to engage them in reading rather than to insist that they build up to reading by first learning sounds. Of course, learning sounds is important, and the professional dispute between phonics and whole-language methods is largely silly. The child needs both, but, most importantly, she needs an engagement with a meaningful narrative. The same holds for other subjects: Arithmetic and grammar are cases in point.

Dewey also wants to stress that this is not just a one-way street where the teacher teaches and the child learns. In a meaningful educational engagement, both have certain competencies, and both are learning and undergoing change. For example, Dewey does not believe that teachers can ignore the methods developed over time and used by experienced practitioners of an activity. This is a common mistaken interpretation of Dewey's ideas. Just as future artists must learn to use the tools, techniques and methods of accomplished contemporary and past artists, learning involves mastering the methods that more experienced practitioners have mastered. But mastery means the capacity to *use*, not just copy. You master a language by using it. As it is being mastered you can say more complicated things, read more interesting material and write your own story in your own way. Mastery promotes individuality and uniqueness.

The Difference Between Copy and Use

Once in the 1980s when I was doing research in Japan, I visited an English class in a high-pressure Japanese cram school that helps students pass the entrance examination for a high-prestige university. The class had about 300 students, all men, each one sitting in a neat row with the teacher, almost invisible, behind a high podium in the front of the room. Most all of the class was conducted in Japanese, except for a few English phrases that the instructor muttered once in a while, for example: "Step into the bus"; "step out of the car." I doubt whether the students were learning more than a technical understanding of arcane features of grammar. The contrast was a small class of a dozen or so women training to be lower-level secretaries or travel agents. Their classroom was nicely carpeted and cozy, and the students were all engaged in discussing *in English* an American novel. These students were not only learning English. They were also learning to appreciating it as a mode of expression and communication.

Dewey believed that "[w]hen engaged in the direct act of teaching, the instructor needs to have subject matter at his fingers' end; his attention should be upon the attitude and response of the students ... Hence simple scholarship is not enough."[10] The teacher needs to understand the logic of the subject, but not *just* from the point of view of the expert, but also from the logic and interest of the student. (I agree with Dewey, but I also question whether the limited number of years of teacher training could be sufficient to develop this level of expertise.)

The Logic of the Child

Let me give a simple example of the logic of the child. A second-grade child kept losing his place in music class. He was singing the words of one stanza in the music book when he should have been singing words of another. After listening to the student, the teacher figured out that the child was reading one line after another, as he was taught to do in reading text. A simple correction resolved the problem. The child was applying logic appropriate for one kind of narrative to another.

The example should make one suspicious of research that claims that class size does not make a difference without taking into account the background of the students and the purpose of the class. Perhaps in situations where students come from a very similar background and share a good deal of tacit understanding, size will matter somewhat less than in a situation where students come from very different backgrounds and do not share the same body of tacit understanding. In the case of the music class, it certainly did matter that the teacher had a small enough class that she could listen to the singing of an individual child. "As a teacher one has to interpret the child's behavior in the light of the adult-developed refined curriculum, and the curriculum in the light of the child."[11]

Commentary: Revisiting the Question of Doubt

In an earlier chapter, I noted the important role that doubt plays in thinking for Dewey and other pragmatists. Dewey does not say a great deal about how doubt is developed except to note that it arises out of a problematic situation. But it is unlikely that doubt just arises naturally. Problematic situations have to be recognized as *problematic* before doubt occurs. The development of a disposition to doubt and to be conscious of that doubt is itself an educational task and it is not easy to accomplish in many cases. Part of the task of the teacher is then to construct an environment where doubt could arise.

The process of education involves the development of a disposition to question and to shake certainty. But certainty itself is often satisfying and can be the result of some success. To learn to doubt for Dewey is part of learning to think, but developing a disposition to doubt is complicated because closure, or satisfaction is also a part of the process of education. It provides students with a platform from which doubt can proceed. Yet for education to advance, satisfaction must be destabilized to a certain extent. Here is where the teacher's role as a bridge between the novice and the expert comes into play. Part of the function of teaching is to destabilize satisfaction by encouraging the student to explore the limitations of the practice that brings satisfaction.

Take learning to ski as an example. One of the most difficult maneuvers in skiing is learning how to stop. Now there are two techniques that beginners use. The first is to sit on one's butt and hope that you don't hit an ice patch. But this way is awkward and its limitation obvious. While it can be somewhat effective way to stop in some situations, it is inefficient. It is exhausting to get up each time, and you might hit an icy patch. A second and somewhat more effective way is called the snowplow. Here you put your skis in a "V" shape and use the edges to build up the snow so that its resistance will stop you. If you are lucky, you will not fall and can simply start again. The snowplow is a solution to the problematic situation—how do I get these things to stop? The problem is that it too is an extremely inefficient way to stop, and turning is very awkward using this method, requiring a large arc.

Ski instructors may construct experiences that underscore the problems with the snowplow as a way to motivate students to adopt a more effective method of stopping, the christie. Here, the instructor builds up doubt by introducing expectations that the old method cannot fulfill. Each new expectation involves a new and more complex problematic situation and the development of a new and more efficient method of performing the task. A similar process occurs in learning a musical instrument. Lots of different techniques will enable the student to play "Twinkle, Twinkle," but some of these will inhibit advancement to, say playing Bach, unless they are corrected, forgotten and changed. This is a far cry from those "child-centered" educators who simply allow children to express their own interest, or who want only to build up their self-confidence by telling them what a good job they are doing. Of course, it is also a far cry from the perfectionist who insists on nothing less than the expert method to begin with. Yet the music example raises problems for Dewey's idea that the skiing example does not.

In skiing, it is relatively easy for the novice to see the limitation of his present method of stopping. Watch out for that tree! A lot of the skiers around her can do it more effectively using the christie. So she might be motivated to practice, via rote if necessary, the steps needed to master the new move and abandon the snowplow. Learning to play an instrument presents a different kind of problem. The student might play "Twinkle, twinkle" just fine. However, the way she holds the bow will not enable her to perform some of the more complicated movements that, say, Bach will require. But Bach is so far in the future that the instructor may simply need to correct the student's bow and tell her to practice the new move, but without any clear reason as to the advantage of doing so. In fact, the new method of holding the bow may well result in a less pleasant "Twinkle, Twinkle." In this case, a certain amount of blind trust—no doubt—may be critical for growth in technique.

For Dewey, the logic of the child or novice is not to be understood as inferior but as different. When the child in the music class read the stanzas sequentially, she was not wrong in some global way. She was simply applying a strategy that she had learned to apply in one situation to another where it does not work. To understand what is happening, the teacher needs to adjust her own frame in order to see the reasoning behind the child's performance. It is critical for teachers to grasp the particular way in which a child is competent if she is to truly respect the child's performance and not just to fake it.

Today, the relatively new field of situated cognition begins with the assumption that people are competent and then explores the way that this competence is manifested in different spheres of life. A mother without a high school degree is able to estimate her grocery bill and to keep to her budget, while a Nobel Prize-winning physicist has difficulty balancing her checkbook. The poorest reader in a class has managed to decode the novice teacher's method for calling on students to read and uses that knowledge to protect herself from the embarrassment of public failure by assuring that she is never called upon.[12] Knowing that the child fears embarrassment, the seasoned teacher takes steps to avoid embarrassing her while still helping her to learn how to read. Once the child understands the teacher will protect her from embarrassment, this trust is easier.

By engaging the child's interest, the teacher encourages curiosity and initiative, promoting engaged learning. Dewey felt that it was critically important that positive and negative emotions followed from the engagement of the child with the activity itself and not from some outside force as an external reward or punishment. Teaching a child to hear her own music performance or to feel her how her legs feel when she executes the christie for the first time can be very effective in teaching the student to monitor and improve her own performance. For Dewey, this was not only a critical component of development; it was also an imperative for democracy.

The School and Social Progress

There is some question as to whether Dewey changed his understanding of schooling over time. His early optimism that schools could be at the forefront of progressive change was developed at a time of increasing immigration and as the country was changing from a rural, farming society to an urban, industrial one. Moreover, his *My Pedagogical Creed* (1897), an early work where he saw teachers as prophets of democracy, was published before compulsory education to the age of sixteen was universal. While he may never have lost hope that the school would become the principle agent of progressive social change, his last major work on Education, *Experience and Education* (1938) was more critical of certain progressive practices and is often seen as attempting to correct the balance between the progressive's emphasis on the interests of the child and the traditionalists concern with the importance of the subject matter.

In point of fact, Dewey always acknowledged the importance of both attending to the child and to the curriculum, the title of one of his books, but at different times he would highlight one over the other. Hence, for example, the *Child and the Curriculum* (1902) and *School and Society* (1907), both drawn from his time as the director of the Laboratory School at the University of Chicago, describe and justified the work that went on in that school, and its activity-centered approach to learning. After he left Chicago and the Lab School, Dewey continued to write about education and to develop his ideas about its relation to democracy. In *Democracy and Education* (1916), Dewey's most comprehensive work on education, he conceptualizes in more detail the characteristics of a democratic education.

Growth

The aim of education, Dewey tells us, is growth. Dewey does not say what the end of growth is, save more growth, but he does give a clear idea of the role that it serves in human development, and in education. To begin with, Dewey makes the seemingly obvious point that the condition of growth is immaturity, which does not mean simply incapacity, but also a real and existing capacity. Interestingly, Dewey finds this existing capacity in the child's exceptional power to "enlist the cooperative attention of others."[13] For example, the quickness by which a child can get an adult to respond to its laugh or cry is an expression of this power. As Dewey puts it, "human infants . . . can get along with physical incapacity just because of their social capacity."[14] They are born with a remarkable capacity for social intercourse. Consider, for example, all of the energy a baby can elicit from a parent as she undertakes to learn how to walk. "From a social standpoint, dependence denotes a power rather than a weakness; it involves interdependence."[15]

Now, this interdependence is not only a feature of infants and children, it a mark of both education and democracy. As we grow, we not only learn to take advantage of the capacities of other people, we also, I suggest, become conscious of doing so. One of the implications of this is that a democracy is an arrangement where its members are mutually aware of their interdependence and where they are concerned about maintaining and enhancing conditions of mutual growth. Hence, Dewey characterizes education as "the enterprise of supplying the conditions which insure growth, or adequacy of life, irrespective of age."[16]

Dewey does not spell out what this interdependence means in any great detail, but I suggest that it would entail the awareness on the part of each individual member of the conditions for the adequate participation of every other member. For example, feminist educational research has documented the unequal rates of participation of girls and boys in classrooms and has suggested methods of increasing the rate of participation of girls. This work is consistent with Dewey's view that

> [t]he purpose of school education is to insure the continuance of education by organizing the powers that insure growth. The inclination to learn from life itself and to make the conditions of life such that all will learn in the process of living is the finest product of schooling.[17]

Education is the process of social renewal where both social skills and values are reproduced in each new generation and where each new generation comes to share in the interest of growth for themselves and each other and for of the group as a whole, including future generations. *Democracy and Education* serves as a roadmap for reconnecting learning and interest in different subject matter areas and in schools as a democratic institution where systematic inquiry is used to enable society to self-consciously change itself.

Growth involves adaptation, but adaptation, as conceived by Dewey, is not a passive affair where the environment is fixed and the person is expected to change to fit it. Adaptation involves a transactional relationship of a person with an environment where both undergo change. It involves the capacity to change the environment as well as the capacity to change our own characteristic responses to that environment and the nature of our interest in it. Just as the skier grows out of the snowplow into the christie and seek new challenges, our interests change and grow. We can be subjugated by both an environment that overwhelms us as well as by habits that confine us to rigid, unbending responses. Careful observation, imagination, reflection, conscious deliberation and experimentation in response to problematic situations involving both person and environment are the corrective to both an unyielding environment and unbending habits. "Learning from experience" means more than just having a lot of different experiences. For Dewey, it means the developed capacity to use inquiry to modify action by reference to the consequences of past actions and to the possibility for better results in the future.

A Closer Look at Dewey's Ideas on Democracy and Education

Jane Addams (1860–1935), largely known as one of the founders of the field of social work, was a close friend and confidant of Dewey. Addams, along with Dewey's first wife, Harriet Alice (Chipman) Dewey, helped Dewey become see the importance of social action to democratic formation. Moreover, his definition of democracy, like Addams's, places human associations rather than political parties at the center of democracy. As Addams critically wrote of political reformers: "In trying to better matters they have in mind only political achievements which they detach in a curious way from the rest of life, and they speak and write of the purification of politics as a thing apart from life."[18]

In *Democracy and Education*, Dewey draws on Addams's idea of democracy and makes it the central plank in his educational theory. For him, democracy is less about the rules of government than it is about the quality of association. This is formalized in his standard for democratic groups: "How numerous and varied are the interests which are consciously shared? How full and free is the interplay with other forms of association."[19]

He identifies democracy as a "mode of associated living, of conjoint communicative experience,"[20] where there is an ever "widening of the area of shared concerns, and the liberalization of a greater diversity of personal capacities."[21] In other words, democracy involves a community that nourishes individual growth and diversity. Democracy in Dewey's formulation stands against the isolation of individuals and groups, and especially those groups that breed rigidity and fear of any interaction with members of other groups.[22] For Dewey, this understanding of democracy provides the grounds for an education that does not center authority exclusively in one person, the teacher. Rather, the teacher's role in a democratic classroom is to construct an environment where individual interests are shaped and developed and opportunities are provided for cooperative, interactive learning to take place. As Dewey puts it:

> The extension in space of the number of individuals who participate in an interest so that each has to refer his own action to that of others, and to consider the action of others to give point and direction to his own, is equivalent to the breaking down of those barriers of class, race, and national territory which kept men from perceiving the full import of their activity.[23]

Here, Dewey's idea might refer to a nation-state which promotes diversity and inclusion, or it could also refer to smaller units: Think, for example, of how a jazz ensemble or a successful basketball team might function with each player contributing their own individual talent while taking into account the movements of the other, and where that talent is enhanced as it adds to the group effort.

> These more numerous and more varied points of contact denote a greater diversity of stimuli to which an individual has to respond; they consequently put a premium on variation in his action. They secure a liberation of powers which remain suppressed as long as the incitation to action are partial, as they must be in a group which in its exclusiveness shuts out many interests[24]

While Dewey's understanding of democracy is today correctly associated with contemporary theories of deliberative democracy, there is a distinction to be made between sharing an interest on the one hand and deliberating and coming to agreement about a course of action on the other. The latter is the crux of the idea of deliberative democracy. Certainly Dewey is aware of these distinctions at some level. He did believe that the interpenetration of interests is a condition of both deliberation and self-government.[25] However he does not make the distinction explicit leaving him open to criticism from the left that his formulation invites the manipulation of interests. However without dismissing this concern I suspect his reasoning went something like this: If we differ about one issue perhaps, we can agree about many others, and then, hopefully, this larger area of agreement will minimize the negative impact of our differences and promote new and more encompassing interests. This is related to deliberative conceptions of democracy, where one of the things that we deliberate about is our differences and how they can be addressed.

Questions About Dewey's Conception of Democracy

Dewey's makes the philosophical case for his conception of democracy in Chapter Seven of *Democracy and Education* and concludes that democracy can be measured by "[h]ow numerous and varied are the interests which are consciously shared? How full and free is the interplay with other forms of association?"[26]

One of the significant features of Dewey's conception of democracy is just how little it relies on traditional arguments that were available to him at the time. He largely ignores Locke's view that all legitimate government rests on the consent of the governed, as well as Madison's view on democracy and the separation of powers or Mill's argument for liberty and the argument for a minimum state that performs only those necessary functions that private enterprises are unlikely to serve at affordable costs. Ignoring these theories enables Dewey to develop a more expansive notion of the role of public institutions such as the school, while, at the same time, it allows him to favor certain kinds of groups over others, namely those that fit his conception of democracy. But it makes an important difference as to whether Dewey intended his conception of democracy to complement or to replace the traditional ones.

This question is important, because replacing these more traditional definitions may come at a price. Dewey does not address the rights of those members of groups that may not fit his more expansive conception, for example, orthodox Jewish groups or fundamentalist Christians, or some indigenous groups that want to restrict the legitimate interests of their members as well as the association of members of their group with members of other groups. Even while non-democratic in terms of their own members, they need not be anti-democratic in terms of objecting to the exercise of rights to freedom of association or speech for non-members. If Dewey were simply assuming the validity of the traditional theories and then offering his own theory as a supplemental add-on, then this would be one thing. However, if he were offering his own view as a substitute for the more traditional idea about democracy, then that would be quite another.

Granted Dewey's conception is consistent with the right of free association, after all, that is part of his definition of democracy. It also may suggest a view of rights that might go beyond simply political rights. For example, the rights to medical care or food might apply to Dewey's understanding of democracy more than to, say that of John Locke or Thomas Jefferson. If intended as a substitute to traditional political democracy, however, the question might be raised as to whether the conception of democracy he offers provides sufficient protection for basic rights, such as the right to be left alone or of the right to associate only with like-minded people. My own view is that Dewey's conception of democracy works best in the context of education but is wanting in the context of politics.

There is also the question of whether his emphasis on *the number and variety of interests shared* neglects the quality of those interests. It is doubtful that Dewey would approve of, say, a gang of thieves, some of whom also played basketball, others of whom sang in barbershop quartets, while still others collected outsider art etc. In addition, Mill's argument against Bentham's utilitarian formula that the good equals the greatest pleasure for the greatest number might apply to Dewey as well. In contrast to Bentham, Mill thought that some pleasures were of a "higher" quality than others. Perhaps some interests are also higher than others. Granted, Mills's formulation does have elitist implications, and a Deweyian might object by saying: Who are you to tell me that your interest in, say, Beethoven is of a higher quality than my interest in Broadway musicals? However, there is a less elitist way to express this criticism by noting that not all worthwhile interests are compatible. The muscles that a tennis player needs to develop are not the same as the ones required by a linebacker, and these are not compatible with those needed by a ballet dancer.

Now, these concerns may be addressed in two ways. The first is to recall that Dewey's remarks on democracy are imbedded in his major book on education and that much of what he says about democracy must be understood in light of other chapters about the aims of *education*. Chapter Seven is the link between Dewey's understanding of *education* as a social function and the role of formal *schooling* in promoting certain ways of understanding and relating to each other. Second, as suggested previously, he should have made a distinction between political democracy and educational democracy. Political democracy would concede that a good society must enable people to be idiosyncratic, even non-social, while educational democracy requires the development of a capacity for social engagement. Obviously, this distinction is not absolute, and critical questions arise about say parents' rights to educate children into their own preferred way of life, even if that way of life is not especially democratic. Perhaps the most reasonable way to read Dewey's formula on democracy is not as a rule or a formula at all, but as a heuristic encouraging exploration and risk.

Continuing Relevance of Dewey's Educational Ideas

In recent years, there has been a growing emphasis on educational assessment, standardized tests and accountability. To the extent that Dewey is seen as promoting more scientific public accountability, this emphasis is consistent with his ideas. However, to the extent that his work is associated with respect for children's creativity and the uniqueness of their individual experience, an emphasis on standardized tests and lock step accountability is problematic. Much will depend on whether these new reforms promote more than test-taking skills and whether they actually encourage connections between thinking and experience and whether they advance the cooperative democratic community that Dewey had in mind. Today, the picture is certainly not encouraging.

An Example From Japan: The Tension Between Growth and Accountability

I recall, for example, a visit to a school in Japan, where the teacher described to me two kinds of science classes that he taught. The students in the first were expected to take the highly standardized test in science required for entrance to many of the high status high schools at the time. Students in the second, many of whom had been abroad with their parents for part of their education, had the science test requirement waived. The teacher was very excited about the second class and described to me how the students were learning science by collecting specimens from the pond in the back of the school and spending weeks analyzing their development, drawing hypothesis, testing them out and drawing conclusions. He felt that they were truly learning science by connecting thinking and experience in the way that Dewey suggested. I then asked about the second group, the one that was expected to take the high-stakes test. His response was simple and direct. "I can't teach them science, they are too busy learning how to pass the test."

Notes

1. John Dewey, "My Pedagogical Creed," *School Journal*, 54 (January 1897), pp. 77–80.
2. John Dewey, *The School and Society/The Child and The Curriculum* (Chicago: University of Chicago Press, 1990), pp. 11–12.
3. Joseph Mayer. Rice, "The Public Schools of Chicago and St. Paul," *The Forum*, 15 (April 1893), pp. 206–208.
4. Joseph Mayer Rice "The Public School System of New York City," *The Forum*, 14 (January 1892), p. 617.
5. John Dewey, *Democracy and Education* (New York: The Free Press, 1916), p. 141.
6. Ibid., p. 169.
7. John Dewey, *The School and Society/The Child and the Curriculum* (Chicago: The University of Chicago Press, 1990), pp. 6–7.
8. Dewey, "My Pedagogical Creed."
9. Dewey, *Democracy and Education*, p. 169.
10. Ibid., p. 183.
11. My appreciation to Eric Bredo for this wording.
12. Herve Varenne and Ray McDermott, *Successful Failure* (Boulder, CO: Westview, 1998).
13. Dewey, *Democracy and Education*, p. 43.
14. Ibid.
15. Ibid., p. 44.
16. Ibid., p. 51.
17. Ibid.
18. Jane Addams, *Democracy and Social Ethics* (New York: Macmillan Co., 1902), p. 223.

19. Dewey, *Democracy and Education*, p. 83.
20. Ibid.
21. Ibid.
22. Ibid., p. 86.
23. Ibid., p. 87.
24. Ibid.
25. Ibid.
26. Ibid.

5

TOWARD A NEW PROGRESSIVE EDUCATIONAL MOVEMENT

> When I say that the first object of a renascent liberalism is education, I mean that its task is to aid in producing the habits of mind and character, the intellectual and moral patterns, that are somewhat near even with the actual movement of events.
>
> John Dewey, *Liberalism and Social Action*[1]

In this chapter, I address the question Dewey raised in his book *Liberalism and Social Action* and ask just what are the habits of mind and character, the intellectual and moral patterns that would be somewhat near the actual movement of events as we are experiencing them today in the first quarter of the twenty-first century. I also suggest ways in which a renascent progressive education could contribute to the construction of those habits of mind and character.

The Social Imaginary of Optimism

In the first chapter, I introduced Charles Taylor's concept of a social imaginary. To recapitulate briefly, a social imaginary is an implicit worldview that people draw upon in understanding and communicating to one another. It delineates collective expectations and aspirations and shapes their normative standards.

In 1944, Gunnar Myrdal, the Swedish economist, captured much of this idea of imaginary by his description of the "American Creed" as a commitment to the "essential dignity of the individual human being, of the fundamental equality of all men, and of certain inalienable rights to freedom, justice, and a fair opportunity."[2] In addition to this set of beliefs, the imaginary of optimism and trust also presupposed that things are moving in the right direction—in this case, toward that "more perfect union." Pragmatism's promotion of science as the engine of desirable social change belongs to this imaginary. Dewey's understanding of progressive education and his faith that schools could produce the requisite habits of mind, character, intellect and morality that this creed required was also part of this imaginary.

Myrdal, quoting Ralph Bunch, the African American political scientist, diplomat and future Nobel Peace Prize winner, captures the prevalence of this Creed.

> "Every man in the street, white, black, red or yellow, knows that this is "the land of the free," "the land of opportunity," "the cradle of liberty," "the home of democracy," that the American flag symbolizes the "equality of all men" and guarantees to us all "the protection of life, liberty and property," freedom of speech, freedom of religion and racial tolerance.[3]

I doubt that every man in the street *knew* that this "was the land of the free." Nevertheless, the very fact that, without a hint of irony, Myrdal quotes Bunch, who, despite his accomplishments, would have been confined to the back of the train or, worse, lynched for approaching a white woman as an equal anywhere below the Mason-Dixon line, illustrate just how pervasive was this Creed. It served, though, not as a picture of the real world, but rather as an aspiration about what that world could and would become.

Dewey and the Imaginary of Trust and Optimism

Dewey's educational philosophy both drew on an imaginary of trust, hope and optimism and contributed to it. His goal was to promote the qualities of mind and the character traits required by both scientific inquiry and a democratic society. Students would develop the skills and dispositions required to examine competing courses of action and the capacities required to cooperatively solve scientific, social and environmental problems. A *democratic education would help children learn* to work together to shape a social and natural environment where human growth would be the norm.

For Dewey, a democratic education enlarges meaning and expands community. It draws on the active interests of individual students and connects them to the larger historical community. It helps students develop the skills they will need to shape their futures and to actively participate in shaping the direction of society. A democratic education provides future citizen with multiple points of connections with each other. It enables them to develop new interests and association. An autocratic authority, whether practiced in traditional schools or in paternalistic families, Dewey thought was anathema to this ideal.

Dewey on the Meaning of Americanization

Dewey was an advocate of educational diversity long before the word entered the politically correct lexicon. He argued that individual and social growth depended on novelty, on the extension of existing interests and on the development of new ones. Diversity of interest, environment and individual talent introduced novelty and thus was a condition of individual and communal growth. However, his emphasis was not on ethnic or gender diversity as much as it was on economic diversity. He believed that the largest impediment to diverse educational experiences was the rigid class lines that prevented "the adequate interplay of experience."[4] He saw this rigidity as a trademark of classical capitalism.

In fact, progressives differed on what should be done about ethnic diversity. Dewey occupied a middle ground between two poles. The first pole was represented by President Woodrow Wilson, a political progressive, who held that there should be one single American identity that overrode any other allegiance. The other pole was represented by cultural progressives like Horace Kallen (1882–1974), a Jewish American philosopher. In contrast to Wilson, Kallen held that American pluralism must acknowledge the uniqueness of each individual culture. He believed that each national immigrant group had its own distinctive emotional register and its own aesthetic forms, which he felt were most genuinely expressed in their own unique language. (African American philosophers like Alain Locke and W. E. B. Du Bois, both of whom explored the particular experience and contribution of black culture, also developed the idea that the experience and values of each individual culture was unique.) Kallen felt that whereas in Europe, these differences often resulted in national conflict, he argued that America provided an environment where each culture could add its voice to the other in a peaceful way, thus maintaining their own unique identity.

Dewey sympathized with Kallen's views but was skeptical of the idea that immigrant group members, many of whom had been antagonists to each other in Europe, could exist peacefully in America without significant educational intervention. Left to their own devices, he believed that these groups would reproduce their European conflicts in America and would maintain antagonistic relations and reinforce old autocratic habits. He also feared that such habits would lead to the exploitation of the newest immigrants both by members of their own group and by unscrupulous native politicians. Dewey saw progressive schooling to be a prerequisite for individual growth and social harmony and a democratic America.

For Dewey, the flourishing of the individual and the flourishing of a democracy required the same things: novelty, diversity, reflection and experimentation. Individuals grow when old habits are challenged by new conditions. Societies grow when they are able to intelligently adapt to a changing environment and to direct it in productive ways through reflection, inquiry and science. Communities grow when their members can freely intermingle with members of other communities. Dewey observed that every aspect of the environment—natural, physical, technological, social and cultural—was undergoing a profound change, and he believed that change required new modes of control and development if it were to proceed in a humane and productive way. He believed that cultural groups were valuable and that working together, they could participate in the co-construction of an emerging cultural identity.

Limitations

Dewey's educational ideas have always been controversial. The criticisms include the friendly assessment by the philosopher

Israel Scheffler, who contended that subject matter can generate its own interest without attaching itself to an already present interest that students brings with them to the subject. Scheffler believed that intellectual problems embedded in complex theory can be sufficient to generate an interest in some students where none had existed before. In other words, teaching students complex theory does not always require a preexisting interest that needs to be corralled into learning a worthwhile subject.[5] I believe that Scheffler is quite right and that Dewey overemphasizes the need to colonize a preexisting interest.

Another criticism offered by E. D. Hirsch, Jr. is that progressive education is inefficient and that students often can learn more efficiently by direct instruction where the teacher lays out the larger ideas, concepts or methods that need to be learned and where learning is then reinforced by practice, which might include drill, recitation, and memorization. Hirsch also has a point, although he fails to see the important connection Dewey makes between the how—or method of instruction- and the what—or the subject that is learned (see Chapter 4). The criticism of Dewey also includes more hostile critics from the political right, who irrationally blame Dewey for the decline of the national moral character and for misunderstanding the educational prerequisites of philosophy.[6]

A few theologians, such as Reinhold Niebuhr, rightly questioned Dewey's core optimism, and the journalist Walter Lippmann challenged Dewey's faith in *open and transparent* inquiry. However, for the most part, Dewey's belief that the scientific method, extended to social affairs, could resolve even the most intransient of human problems fit nicely with the social imaginary of the times and was consistent with the growth of the social sciences. From the 1920s through the 1950s, Dewey's ideas were at the forefront of the liberal left.

This changed dramatically in the late 1960s and early 1970s as then newly named "old left"—Dewey's liberals—gave way to a less positive "new left." This change was more than generational—"Don't trust anyone over 30," the cry of the new left in 1970—it was also intellectual, marking a challenge to both political authority and to intellectual authority, including that of Dewey.

From a Social Imaginary of Optimism to a Social Imaginary of Suspicion

The educational philosopher, George Counts, delivered his famous "Dare the Schools Build A New Social Order" speech in 1931, before the Progressive Education Association. In it, he expressed the optimism that schools could be a significant agent of progressive change even in the midst of the worst economic depression in history. Of course, there were different responses at the time, but these were largely about the merits of indoctrinating students into the new social order as opposed to finding ways to letting them come to the *right* conclusion by themselves, conclusions that many progressives confidently professed to know. Even the Communist party in New York thought that a voice in the schools was sufficiently important that they contested with more liberal members, including Dewey, for control of the union.

It is the response to Counts's question "Can the school build a new social order?" that divided the 1930 educational progressives from the New Left of the 1970s. By the 1970s, the imaginary of the left had changed from one of basic trust that the schools could be a force for progressive change to one of deep distrust. The change is illustrated by contrasting the hope generated after the *Brown v. Board of Education* decision in 1954 which ended legal segregation to the white reaction against bussing in the late 1960s and early 70s even in such "liberal" enclaves as my hometown, Boston. All of this had an impact on my own work and the way I began to read Dewey in the late 1960s and early 1970s.

Some Background

I was born almost eighty years after Dewey. He was still alive and actively engaged in politics, education and philosophy when I was learning to walk. He was witness to the Great Depression from its beginning. I was born just before it ended. We both were alive, he, eighty-six, me, eight, when the atomic bombs were dropped and the Second World War ended. He died when the Korean War (1950–1953) was at its height and when my own political awareness was beginning to waken and just as Richard Nixon was coming into national prominence. By the time television brought the Army McCarthy hearings into my home in 1954, Dewey had passed away. In that same year, *Brown v. Board of Education* was decided, and segregated schools were ruled unconstitutional.

Growing up in Boston in the 1940s and 50s, it was not too hard to condemn the legally segregated conditions of the South as a violation of the basic idea of equal opportunity, an idea that Dewey had championed throughout his life. It was a lot harder for me to realize just how normalized segregation and inequality was in the North. There were no African American students in my *legally* unsegregated grade school. When my high school asked for volunteers to house the single African American band member from another school, my family was the only one to volunteer. But these were only the outer trappings of informal apartheid; the inner ones were more difficult to identify until they hit you in the face. And so my surprise was palpable when a Boston department store in the mid-1960s finally put a black manikin in its display window. It was also palpable a few years later in Champaign when I had to bring our young daughter to the emergency room and I mistook the black female emergency room *doctor* for the nurse and the white male *nurse* for the doctor.

Dewey did not likely experience the full impact of these changes, allowing his generation—at least those of white European origin—to take the idea of American exceptionalism for granted. For my own family, some of whom had come to America to escape the pogroms in Russia and some others who would have been murdered in the Holocaust had they remained in Europe, America was, for all its many faults, exceptional. But this was not true for everyone. The story of slavery, of Native American genocide, of the takeover of Mexican land was told, if told at all, from the point of view of slave owners and conquerors. The Vietnam War, the Civil Rights movement, the assassinations of President Kennedy, Malcolm X, Dr. King, Medgar Evers and Robert Kennedy, the Watergate hearings, all marked a change in the dominant social imaginary and the consciousness of my generation. At stake was the very idea of American exceptionalism and of progress itself.

This was the real dividing point between Dewey's generation and those that followed mine. I was in the middle, having internalized much that Dewey had also internalized—the promise of public education for a more inclusive, more democratic society, and yet I was also standing outside of Dewey's generation and questioning much that it took for granted—including the belief that schooling could achieve greater equality by itself.

This change was consistent with the development of a new social imaginary, suspicion and distrust, born of the violence that met civil rights workers and of the slaughter of the Vietnam War. Vietnam was more than a tragic mistake. The over three million Vietnamese and 58,000 American deaths terminated whatever remained of America's self-congratulatory innocence. The lesson of Watergate was not just that the government makes mistakes, which Dewey certainly knew, but that it lies and that it does so systematically and impartially by Democrats and Republics alike. Watergate and Vietnam reframed the social imaginary from optimism and trust to suspicion and distrust.

The Struggle on Campus

At the time in the late 1960s and early 1970s, the faculty of the University of Illinois Urbana Champaign College of Education was divided between young Turks, like myself, and the older, more established faculty members. One of my senior colleagues, a Dewey scholar, loudly called me a traitor at a party because of my opposition to the War in Vietnam, and he later chalked a Swastika on my office door. After the murders of students at Kent and Jackson State, I, and others, spoke in favor of a resolution for a campus boycott to protest the war. A day or so after the resolution was passed, a top administrator called me into his office to tell me that if I wanted to change the world, the university was no place for me. I later found out that he gave the same message to other protesting faculty. After Watergate and after the government duplicity became undeniable, it seemed to me that both the colleague who thought me a traitor and the administrator who questioned my place in the university, along with much of the nation itself, softened their opposition to the resistance, with some joining it.

The Changing Social Imaginary

Behind these charges and counter charges were two competing views about the proper relationship between power and intelligence, interpreted then as the government and the professoriate. The old left held that intelligence could still be linked to power to serve the public good, even though some eventually came to question the wisdom of the Vietnam War. The new left held that power corrupted intelligence and that resistance was the only viable form of effective action. The slogan "don't trust anybody over 30," popular at the time, implied that power corrupts, older people are prone to cooptation by power and only distrust and resistance, qualities of the young, purify. The Watergate scandal was not alone in convincing many people, even some over thirty, that engagement with the government corrupts. It was reinforced by earlier revelations about the cooperation between academics—psychologists, anthropologists, economists—and the Department of Defense to overthrow democratically elected regimes in other countries and promote a pro-American business policy.

The conflict was about both legitimacy and meaning. To illustrate this, consider the two closely related terms—cooperation and cooptation—and their implication. The first, of course, is essential to Dewey's political and educational philosophy and is foundational to his ideas about both democracy and *democratic* education. It relies on the social imaginary of trust and optimism. When you decide to cooperate with someone else, you assume that the conditions for true cooperation are present, trust, good will, transparency and a reasonably equal balance of power. Cooptation holds that these conditions are not present and that the call for cooperation is bogus.

When these conditions are thought to be absent, then calls for cooperation will be rightly taken as at attempt at cooptation. Here, the imaginary of trust turns into the imaginary of suspicion and mistrust. The charge of cooptation is not the same as a charge of insincerity. The call for cooperation may be a perfectly sincere one, but if the system itself is corrupt, an otherwise sincere but uniformed call for cooperation will be taken as an attempt at cooptation. This is how things looked to many people in the late 1960s and 70s.

Reading Dewey Under the Imaginary of Suspicion

It was in the context of this shift in the social imaginary that Dewey's Polish Study came to my attention. Dewey had performed the research on a Polish group living in Philadelphia with graduate students and in 1917–18 and submitted the eighty-page report as a confidential document to the War Department in 1918—today the Department of Defense—on the attitudes of this group. A few years before I came across the study when I was writing my dissertation, Dewey's involvement with the Polish Community and the War Department, had not been a topic for Dewey scholars, and I, like most other Dewey scholars, had completely overlooked it . I simply criticized his technical philosophy for failing to address potential conflicts between community and science.

In hindsight, my failure to see the significance of the Polish Study and Dewey's support for the American involvement in the First World War reveals something about my own mindset and about the social imaginary to which it was attuned. I was focused on Dewey's formal *philosophy* and ignored much else. So even though Dewey's study of the Polish Community was marked "confidential" for the War Department in 1918, by 1965, when I finished my dissertation, it was a secret only in the sense that no one had paid any attention to its content, even though it was available to anyone who might be interested and was described fully on pages 52–54 in the then definitive bibliography of Dewey's works.[7]

Given the social imaginary of the early 1970s, the political relevance of the Polish Study to my earlier observation about the tension between intelligence and community in Dewey's thought was now apparent. Dewey had cooperated with the War Department and used social science inquiry to question the loyalty of members of the Polish community. A-hah! Science over community! My criticism was now more than strictly a matter of logic, as it had been in the dissertation; it had become a matter of the meaning of democracy. Or, to put it in terms of the 60s and 70s, Dewey was coopted by the War Department to promote the "cooperation" of the Polish community in advancing American interests as defined by the War Department.

Some of Dewey's former colleagues, such as Jane Addams and Randolph Bourne, remained faithful to their pacifist ideas throughout the war and lamented the extent to which American intellectuals, including Dewey, had supported the war and aided the propaganda supporting it.[8] Addams notes that any opposition during the war was largely silenced by government propaganda, public pressure and by the intellectuals who supported the war. She would likely have had Dewey in mind when she made this remark. He not only came to support the war shortly after it was declared but found a number of occasions to argue against its critics.

Deconstructing the Social Imaginary

A word of clarification about my use of the term social imaginary is in order. The idea of a social imaginary helps us understand the ways in which people make collective sense of their word and the expectations that they share as normal and justifiable. It does not *explain* social change, but is useful in recognizing and labeling it. Nor does it capture the nuances of change, as if we go suddenly from one social imaginary to the next. Certainly there was much distrust in the 1930s, and a lot of people in the 1970s continued to believe that cooperation between academics and government was, on balance, a force for good. The idea of a social imaginary captures a certain tone that pervades discourse and decision-making. It does not explain that change, nor does it weigh how many consciously ascribe to it.

Nor does a change in the social imaginary signal a change in all its parts. The change from the old left to the new was not a rejection of the American Creed as much as it was suspicion about whether it could be achieved under existing conditions. Similarly, the later suspicion and repudiation of the male domination of the new left by feminism drew upon the rhetoric of the new left for equality pointing out how inconsistent it was with its own sexist practices and opening the way for a new set of critiques.

The Social Imaginary, then, is not some massive beast that turns on its parents and devourers them whole. It can be deconstructed, its pieces rearranged and then reconstructed. The imaginary of trust was not overthrown completely by the imaginary of suspicion. There was not for example, a wholesale rejection of the American Creed as a worthy ideal to strive for. Rather, rejected was the idea that it could be achieved by relying on good will alone and reform from above. Dr. King, Rosa Parks, Saul Alinsky, Daniel Ellsberg and, later, Harvey Milk demonstrated the necessity of different forms of non-violent resistance to obtuse, intransigent leaders. Cornell West relates this to Dewey and a limitation in his idea of social change.

"His gradualism is principally pedagogical in content, and his reformism is primarily dialogical in character. He shuns confrontational politics and agitational social struggle" for education and continuous discussion.[9]

The problem is not with education and discussion as such. However, these become problems under conditions of oppression, intransigence and unequal power. Under these conditions, the call for cooperation is to be seen as a ploy to disguise cooptation. And this is what guided much of my own reaction to Dewey's educational writings in the 1970s when I noted his silence on critical race issues such as lynching[10] and segregated schools.[11] The difference was partly about the framework through which subordination was to be understood and whether race had a status independent of social class. But the difference was also about tactics, and the most effective way to promote desirable social change. King, Parks and Alinsky made Dewey's slower, more discursive method less than promising in situations of oppression. As Dr. King put it in his "Letter From a Birmingham Jail":

> I must make two honest confessions to you, my Christian and Jewish brothers. First, I must confess that over the past few years I have been gravely disappointed with the white moderate. I have almost reached the regrettable conclusion that the Negro's great stumbling block in his stride toward freedom is not the White Citizen's Counciler or the Ku Klux Klanner, but the white moderate, who is more devoted to "order" than to justice; who prefers a negative peace which is the absence of tension to a positive peace which is the presence of justice; who constantly says: "I agree with you in the goal you seek, but I cannot agree with your methods of direct action"; who paternalistically believes he can set the timetable for another man's freedom; who lives by a mythical concept of time and who constantly advises the Negro to wait for a "more convenient season." Shallow

> understanding from people of good will is more frustrating than absolute misunderstanding from people of ill will. Lukewarm acceptance is much more bewildering than outright rejection.[12]

King certainly agreed with Dewey about the unity of thought and action, but King's non-violent protest had overtaken Dewey's more cautious, more scientifically inflected approach to change.

> In any nonviolent campaign there are four basic steps: collection of the facts to determine whether injustices exist; negotiation; self purification; and direct action. We have gone through all these steps in Birmingham. There can be no gainsaying the fact that racial injustice engulfs this community. Birmingham is probably the most thoroughly segregated city in the United States. Its ugly record of brutality is widely known. This tactical difference was also a moral difference.

To put it differently, King's words and actions set the social imaginary to a different register—one where inquiry was about tactics and should be a handmaiden to justified protest and resistance. Certainly the difference between King and the liberal moderates was a tactical one, but, as he insisted, it was a moral one as well. Collective power was one ingredient that Dewey underestimated in his call for progressive education.

The Reconstruction of Dewey's Ideas in the Post Modern World: A Fourth Leg for Democratic Education

My criticism of Dewey is itself a part of the pragmatic tradition. It aims to bring together our deepest understanding of democracy, with the facts of social life as we experience them. Clearly, the post-Civil War social imaginary had restricted

Dewey's consideration of the centrality of race in American life. Like most white progressives at the time, for Dewey, racial issues were addressed largely as problems of class. As Glaude remarks: "race and racism remained marginal intellectual categories despite the long, looming shadow of slavery that framed their (James and Dewey) extraordinary lives."[13]

This should not be surprising, given that the very concept of *racism* was largely shaped in the Twentieth Century.[14] Even Dr. King's "March on Washington" was a march for jobs, not just race, and he hoped to include blacks and whites in the struggle for social justice. Dewey was not, of course, oblivious to the treatment of blacks, as his role in the formation of the NAACP attests, but he greatly feared categorizing people in any way that suggested essentialism. He rightly believed that any individual was potentially more than any one classification could encompass, but this belief obscured the very special concerns of subordinated racial populations.

Yet the experience of race as it was revealed to white Americans during the Civil Rights era stripped away the collective myth of American innocence and American perfectibility. And it opened up the possibility of different readings of the American experience—and the need for different voices to be heard through fluid categories of identity, and counter narratives. It also raised the question of power, of who has it and how it is and should be distributed. This suggested a much messier project than that promoted by post-Civil War narratives of national unity or by the older progressive idea of consensus through education and science.

Toward a New Progressive Education

Let's return to the questions I raised (with Dewey) at the beginning of this chapter: What are the habits of mind and character, the intellectual and moral patterns that would be somewhat near the actual movement of events as we are experiencing them today in the first quarter of the twenty-first century, and how might a new form of progressive education contribute to the reconstruction of those habits of mind and character? Dewey believed that the scientific method could be used to advance a progressive agenda, yet he underestimated the extent to which unequal power would be used to distribute the methods and benefits of science unequally.

A new progressive education would recognize structural and systematic inequality and promote more equitable distribution of power. The idea of a new progressive education has three interrelated dimensions. First, it has a political dimension. Students would understand the ways in which benefits are developed and distributed in American society. Second, it has a creative dimension. Students would develop the ethical and aesthetic capacity to imagine alternative realities. Third, it has an academic dimension. Students would develop the scientific, communicative and the *political* skills that promote agency and fulfillment. Here are a few random examples of some of these dimensions.

Recognition of Collective Agency

In the early 1970s, just about the time I read Dewey's Polish Study, I developed a curriculum unit that was centered on the bus boycott that happened in Montgomery in 1955–56 and that spirited Dr. King to national prominence. The unit was inspired by the progressive idea, but had a stronger political content. With the help of a local grade school teacher in a standard elementary school classroom, we developed a group project that required the students to duplicate the boycott using materials we provided and to simulate the problems of the boycott leaders. In doing so, students had to consult demographic materials and to decide effective ways to communicate the boycott to members of the population that could not read newspapers. They had to use maps, news clippings and primary sources to determine where people lived and worked and to then develop car pool routes to take people from their home to their workplace. They also had to figure out how to communicate the boycott to the black population, and, thus, they had to get an idea of how many people could read posters and other notices. For the sizable number of black people in Montgomery who could not read, they had to figure out other modes of communication, such as radio broadcasts and church sermons. They then wrote sermons and developed artwork that promoted the boycott. In the process, students learned map-reading skills, communication skills and organization skills as they learned the role that everyday citizens could play in social change. They also learn a lot about history as they learned about the long history of Civil Rights. With more time or with older students, they might have learned about how textbooks reconstruct history by comparing, say, Rosa Parks's long training at Highlander school to the picture of history text of the tired lady who one day simply decided not to move to the back of the bus. In this unit, students were learning about local efforts to develop collective political agency, but in addition, they were improving basic skills such as literacy, map reading, historical understanding communication and cooperative planning.

Development of Skills of Civic Engagement

The development of communicative and political skills and historical understanding are critical if what Meira Levinson calls the "civic empowerment gap" is to be closed. Civic empowerment involves the knowledge, skills and dispositions that are required to be politically engaged in effective ways. The empowerment gap describes how students differ according to racial, social class and ethnic factors. Levinson argues that racially segregated schools may require a different approach to civic education than do more integrated ones. Empowerment for minority students involves learning and navigating the routes to power within the dominant culture, something more privileged students often learn at home. She believes that effective collective action requires students to learn the ways of the dominant power structure even as they embrace their own traditions. Levinson suggests a number of experiential civic education projects, such as mock trials, community organizing, voter registration drives, collective action about contentious community issues, such as street repair, snow removal and garbage pick-up,[15] that can be used to enhance community engagement and civic empowerment.

Developing a Vision of Renewal

Environmental issues present additional opportunities for students to develop the habits of civic engagement and the moral character that extends beyond any single ethnic identity. One example is the work of Harbor High School in New York. The school, located in Manhattan, is described by its advertising as helping to revitalize the sea life in the harbor by seeding the return of the oyster to New York. Oysters were once abundant in the harbor but became essentially extinct in that body of water and, along with them, much of the ecosystem that sustained sea life. Now students at Harbor High and other schools are working with the project to bring the oyster back, and in the process, they are learning the history and ecology of the bay and using the bay to develop place-based science and math curricula that meet state standards and are applicable to the work of restoring the oyster beds. In learning about the oyster and its role in the development of New York—once, but no longer, one of the largest oyster exporters in the world—the students learn valuable lessons about ecological history, science and math, and they learn too about the effects of human activity on the global as well as the local environment. The opportunity for students from different schools and different communities within a district to come together around a civil concern provides opportunities multicultural, multi-racial and religious cooperation.

Using New Tools to Extend Identity Beyond the Local and National Communities

Finally, the Internet and the World Wide Web make it possible for students to develop interests that transcend local and national boundaries and address issues of global concern. One example at the University of Illinois is the use of the Internet by my colleague, Linda Herrera, to develop a global studies unit on peace education (one of Dewey's major concerns). She was fortunate to be able to draw on two exceptional resources, Raj Gandhi, journalist and a grandson of Mahatma Gandhi, and Mohamed El Baradei, a nuclear weapons inspector and past Egyptian vice president. Both were teaching at the University of Illinois at the time, and both are internationally known for their work on democracy and peace.[16] Herrera was teaching an online course at the time with students enrolled from many different countries. With Gandhi and El Baradei's guidance, the students created a webpage on international and peace issues, and then the students translated it into their different languages, Chinese, Arabic, Korean and Urdu, for others around the world to take advantage of.

Label Warning

We should be cautious about using the labels "progressive education" or "new progressive education," as if they indicated something very different from education pure and simple.[17] The idea of education pure and simple always involves the same things: teach students to be mindful of their environment—natural and social; help students develop respect for each other; encourage them to understand the world that they will inherit as the past's legacy to them and to contribute to the legacy that they will build for future generations. Finally, provide them with the critical intellectual tools that will help them make sound judgments.

There is nothing either uniquely progressive or uniquely traditional about this list, and as Dewey fully appreciated, any education worthy of the name will include both traditional and progressive elements. The ingredients of a good teaching are pretty straightforward. Understand your students, their backgrounds, needs, their interests and their specific talents; understand the subject sufficiently well so that you can teach the requisite skills and engage your students in a critical discussion of inherited points of view; encourage students to test their ideas out and revise them if necessary; and encourage them to become active and engaged members of a community. In addition, as a teacher, learn about the community so that you can communicate with parents and community members about your goals and their children's needs.

As with all lists, this one too is incomplete, but that incompleteness is a mark of any education—progressive, new progressive, traditional—open for revision.

Notes

1. *The Later Works*, 1935–1937 V. 11, *Liberalism and Social Action* (Carbondale: Southern Illinois University Press, 2008), p. 45.
2. Gunnar Myrdal, *An American Dilemma: The Negro in a White America*, Vol. 1 (New York: Harper Row, 1944/1964), p. 4.
3. Ibid., p. 4.
4. John Dewey, *Democracy and Education* (New York: The Free Press, 1916), p. 85.
5. Israel Scheffler, *In Praise of the Cognitive Emotions* (New York: Routledge, 1991), p. 151.
6. See James Scott Johnston, "The Dewey-Hutchins Debate: A Dispute over Moral Teleology," *Educational Theory*, 61 (February 2011), pp. 1–16.
7. Milton Halsey Thomas, *John Dewey: A Centennial Bibliography* (Chicago: The University of Chicago Press, 1929, 1957, 1962), pp. 52–54.
8. Jane Addams, *Peace and Bread in Times of War* (Urbana: University of Illinois Press, 2002), pp. 36–37.
9. Cornell West, *The American Evasion of Philosophy: A Genealogy of Pragmatism* (Madison: The University of Wisconsin Press, 1989), p. 102.
10. Paul C. Taylor, "Silence and Sympathy: Dewey's Whiteness," George Yancy (ed.), *What White Looks Like: African-American Philosophers on the Whiteness Question* (New York: Routledge, 2004), pp. 227–242.
11. Walter Feinberg, *Reason and Rhetoric, the Intellectual Foundations of Twentieth Century Educational Reform* (New York: John Wiley, 1974), pp. 109–110.
12. Martin Luther King, Letter from a Birmingham Jail, April 16, 1863.
13. Eddie S. Glaude Jr., *In A Shade of Blue: Pragmatism and the Politics of Black America* (Chicago: University of Chicago Press, 2007), p. 1 parenthesis mine.
14. Walter Feinberg, *What Is a Public Education and Why We Need It: A Philosophical Inquiry into Self-Development, Cultural Commitment, and Public Engagement* (Lanham: Lexington Books, 2016), pp. 95–112.
15. These are my examples.

16. Gandhi is a grandson of Mahatma Gandhi and is prominent Indian journalist and peace activist in his own right, and Mohamed El Baradei had served as Director of the International Atomic Energy Administration and in that role had refuted the Bush Administration's claim that Iraq had weapons of mass destruction, the rationale used to justify the American invasion of Iraq. Later, during the Egyptian Spring, El Baradei also served, albeit briefly, as his country's vice president.
17. For a lovely exploration of this phrase from a Deweyan point of view see Philip W. Jackson, *What is Education* (Chicago: University of Chicago Press, 2012).

INDEX

accountability 100–101
active learning: authority of the project in 78–79; children and 78–81, 91–92; development of 9–10, 78; in medical education 10; subject matter and pedagogy in 80–81
adaptation 94
Addams, Jane 15, 20, 33, 94–95, 115
Adorno, Theodore xviii
African Americans: Civil Rights movement and 111–112, 119–121; inequality and 111–112; Montgomery bus boycott and 120–121; segregation and 109–110, 117, 122
Alexander, Thomas M. 53
Alinsky, Saul 116–117
American Association of University Professors (AAUP) 15
American Civil War: democracy and 16, 18; disillusionment with God and 20; moral conflicts of 61; plurality of the United States and 17, 61; pragmatic temperament and 26–27; pragmatism and xxii, 4, 14, 17, 21
American Creed 104–105, 116
American exceptionalism 27, 111
Americanization 106–107
American Pragmatism 21

American Psychological Association (APA) 15
analytic philosophy 25–26
analytic truths 25
Aristotle 24
art 39

behavior: character and 57; custom and 56–57; effective action and 55–56; habit and 56; individual 55–56; other-serving 58; social 56–57
beliefs: action and 29; Descartes on 22; James on 29; Locke on 22; Peirce on 24, 30–31; pragmatism and 21–22, 25; truth and 23
Benne, Kenneth xv, xvi, xix, 10
Bentham, Jeremy 99
Berkeley, George 42
Bosanquet, Bernard xix, xx, xxi, xxii
Boston Personalism xiv, xv, xvii, xviii
Bourne, Randolph 115
Bradley, Francis H. xx, xxi
Bredo, Eric 10, 22
Brown v. Board of Education 109–110
Bunch, Ralph 104–105

capitalism: democracy and 16; as a destructive force 33; educational diversity and 106; industrial 33; market xii, xiii

Case, Harold C. xv, xvi
character 57
Child and the Curriculum (Dewey) 92
child-centered education: democratic citizenship and xi, xii; meaning and 39
children: active engagement and xi, 78–81, 91–92; democratic education and 72–74; idealized progressive social change and 82–83; logic of 87; socialization of 74–75; subject matter and 92
Chomsky, Noam 45–46
civic engagement 121–122
civic engagement gap 122
Civil Rights movement 111–112, 119, 121
co-evolution 67–68
Colbert, Stephen 23
collective agency 120–122
collective power 118
communication: community and 52; curriculum unit for 121; democracy as 95; development of 85, 121–122; Locke's view of the mind and 42; meaning and 43, 46, 49–52; social imaginary and 104
community: communication and 52; democratic education and 72, 74, 105–107; meaning and 52; moral 60; schooling and 73–75, 124; socialization and 74–75
compulsory education: enactment of 71, 74, 91; Mann on 1; state laws and 11
concepts 43–44
control 52–54
cooperation: civic engagement and 123; as cooptation 113–114, 117; in learning 96; moral education and 60; oppression and 117; social 33–34; social imaginary of trust and 113–114
cooptation 113–115, 117
Corballis, Michael 52
Counts, George 109

critical theory 26
cultural democracy 4
cultural identity 107
custom 56–58, 60

"Dare the Schools Build a New Social Order" (Counts) 109
Darwin, Charles 16, 20, 32–33
decision-making 63
democracy: American distortion of 2–3; associations in 95–96, 98–99; capitalism and 16; character formation and xi, xviii; cultural 4; defining 95, 97–98; deliberative conceptions of 97; inclusive 16–18; interdependence and 93; meaning and 39; political rights and 4, 98–99; progress toward 3; social action and 95; social construction of xi; social life and 118; systematic inquiry and 4; theories of 97–98
Democracy and Education (Dewey) 10, 78, 83, 92, 94, 95, 97
democratic education: active participation in 73–74; Americanization and 106–107; community and 72–74, 105–107; cooperation and 113; democracy and 1–4, 12, 73, 75; experience and 79–80; Jefferson and 1–2; Mann and 1–2; as street philosophy 2; teacher's role in 95–96; truth-telling and 3
Descartes, René 22, 30–31, 45, 48
Dewey, Alice Greeley 15
Dewey, Harriet Alice Chipman 33, 95
Dewey, John: on co-evolution 67–68; on democracy 95–100; democratic education and 1–3, 12, 95–96; on doubt 88–89; early life and influences 16–20; as ecologist 48; on education 71–83, 85–87, 91–94; on experience 48, 101; humanism and 20–21; influence of xiv, xv, xvi, xvii, 8–11, 15; influence of Darwin on 16, 20, 32–33; on meaning

28, 39–54; on mind 42–43; on moral development 60; on moral education 58–66; as moral relativist 60–62, 66; on moral theory 55–67; post-Civil War influence on 16–18; pragmatism and 14, 20–22, 25–27, 34–35; as public intellectual 14–15, 17, 34; silence on race 117–119; on social cooperation 33–34; social imaginary of 7, 69; support for involvement in World War I 27, 114–115; thought and 22–23, 101

Doi, Takeo 5–6

doubt: Descartes on 30, 48; Peirce on 30–31; problematic situations and 88–89; science and 32

Du Bois, W. E. B. 106

Dunham, Ann 15

economic diversity 106

education: activity-based 9–10, 78–81, 91–92; community and 72, 74, 105–107, 124; copy and use in 86; defining 71, 73; growth and 92–94; industrialization and 75–76; interdependence and 93; liberalism and 103; method in 83; post-Civil War 74–75; preparation in 79; vs. schooling 73; as a social function 99; teachers as experts/novices 85, 87–88; traditional and progressive elements in 124; transformation in 75–76, 91; *see also* democratic education; progressive education

educational democracy 99

educational diversity 106

educational philosophy: influence of Dewey in xix, 10–11; optimism and 105; pragmatism and 25–27; social change and 19; social imaginary and 7; subject matter and pedagogy in 81

educational reform 9

Educational Theory 10

Education and Culture 10

effective action 55–56

El Baradei, Mohamed 123

Ellsberg, Daniel 116

environmental issues 122–123

essential skills 74

ethics: communicative engagement and 50; evolutionary theory of 67–68

ethnic diversity 106–107

European Journal of Pragmatism and American Philosophy, The 11

evil xviii

existentialism xvii, xviii

experience: in democratic education 79–80; growth of the child and 81; meaning and 50; organism/environment interactions and 48

Experience and Education (Dewey) 91

expert knowledge 84–85

feminism 26

freedom xviii

Friedman, Milton xiv

Gandhi, Mahatma 123

Gandhi, Raj 123

Garrison, James 10

Glaude, Eddie S., Jr. 14, 119

global issues 123–124

growth: accountability and 100–101; adaptation and 94; education and 92–94

habit 56, 58, 60

Hegel, Georg W. xviii, xix, 19–21

Hegelian idealism 19–20

Herrera, Linda 123

Hidden Figures 83–84

Hirsch, E. D., Jr. 108

How We Think (Dewey) 59

human improvement: Darwin and 32–33; social cooperation and 33–34

humanism 20

Human Nature and Conduct (Dewey) 55

Hume, David 42

ideas 41–43
individual behavior: character and 57; effective action and 55–56; habit and 56; shared meanings and 57; social side of 56
industrial capitalism 33
industrialization 68, 75
instrumentalism 49
intelligence: power and 113; public good and 113, 115
interdependence: in democracy 93; education and 93; meaning and 48

James, William: infant confusion and 39, 46; influence of 21; on moral theory 68; pragmatic temperament and 26; pragmatism and 14, 20–21, 27–28, 34; on truth 28–29
Jefferson, Thomas: on democracy 98; democratic education and 1–2; slavery and 1, 3
Jeffries, William 10
John Dewey Society 10
Johnson, Katherine Goble 84

Kallen, Horace 106–107
Kant, Immanuel 45–46, 62
Keynes, John M. xiv
King, Martin Luther, Jr. 116–117, 119–120
Knoddings, Nel 10
knowledge 22, 84–85

language 51–52
Laugier, Sandra xvii
learning by doing 79–80
legitimacy 113
"Letter From a Birmingham Jail" (King) 117
Levinson, Meira 121–122
Lewin, Kurt xix
liberalism: defining xii, xiii, xiv; education and 103

Liberalism and Social Action (Dewey) 103
linguistic philosophy: development of 25; influence of xvi, xvii; tasks of xvii
Lippmann, Walter 108
Locke, Alain 106
Locke, John xviii, 22, 41–42, 44, 97–98
Logic (Dewey) 67
Logical Positivism (LP) 44–45
logic of the child 87, 90

Mann, Horace 1–2
market capitalism xii, xiii
Marx, Karl xiii, xviii, 18
Marxism 33
Mead, George Herbert 20
meaning: communication and 42–43, 46, 49–52; community and 52; concepts and 43–44; as confusion to order 39–40, 46–47; control and 52–54; development of shared 52; experience and 45, 48, 50–51; as function and connection 43–44; habits and 47–48; ideas as 41; instrumentalism and 49; interdependence and 48; intersubjective qualities and 45–46; James on 28, 39; language and 51; legitimacy and 113; Logical Positivism (LP) and 44–45; meaningfulness and 53; multi-level 40; notion of means and 49–50; pragmatism and 28–29; as a relationship 46–47; shared 57–58; social system of 53; wholeness and 53–54
meaningfulness 53
medical education 10
Meier, Deborah 10
Menand, Louis xxii, 26
Metaphysical Club, The (Menand) 26
method: subject matter and 81, 83; teachers and 85–86
Milk, Harvey 116

Mill, John Stuart 99
mind: as a blank slate 41–42; Dewey on 22–23, 42–43; Locke on 41–42; as a process 22–23
Montgomery bus boycott 120–121
moral apperception 62
moral claims 61
moral development 60
moral education: development of 60–63; effective thinking and 59; interactions of child and environment in 60; vs. moral miseducation 59; reflection on habits and customs as 58, 60; sense of responsibility and 65; social imaginary 65
moral knowledge 63
moral miseducation 59
moral reasoning 62
moral relativism 60–62, 66
moral theory: critical aspects of 64–65; customs and habits in 56–58; decision-making in 63; effective action and 55–56; everyday life and 62; evolution of 63–68; sense of responsibility and 66; shared meanings and 57–58; social behavior and 57
moral thought 59
Morris, G. Sylvester 19
Murphey, Murray G. 55
My Pedagogical Creed (Dewey) 68, 83, 91
Myrdal, Gunnar 104–105

National Association for the Advancement of Colored People (NAACP) 15, 119
naturalistic fallacy 61
neo-liberalism xii
New Left 109
new liberalism: Dewey on xii, xiii; social change and xiii
Niebuhr, Reinhold 108

non-violent resistance 116, 118
notion of means 49–50

Obama, Barack 15
optimism: educational philosophy and 105; social imaginary of 7, 104–105, 108–109, 113
organism/environment interactions 48
Origin of Species (Darwin) 16
other-serving behavior 58

Paley, Vivian 10
Parker, Francis xi
Parks, Rosa 116–117, 121
peace education 123–124
pedagogy: critical 9; moral message of 58–59; subject matter and 80–81
Peirce, Charles S.: on belief 24, 30–31; on doubt 30–31, 48; influence of 21; pragmatism and 14, 20–21, 34; search for knowledge and 31–32; on truth 29
Personalism ix, x, xvii, xviii
Phillips, Denis 10
Philosophy and the Mirror of Nature (Rorty) 11
Pierce v. Society of the Sisters 11
pluralism: defining xix, xx; democratic xxi; importance of individual cultures in 106–107
Polish Study 114–115, 120
political democracy 4, 98–99
positivism 25
post-modernism 26
power: collective 118; cooperation and 113; corruption and 113; intelligence and 113; minority student empowerment and 122; unequal 120
pragmatism: development of xxii, 4, 14, 21; flourishing of 25; influence of 20–21; James on 27–28; philosophy of xv; as philosophy of action 27; post-Civil War 17, 21; progress and

27; scientific inquiry and 8, 20–21, 30, 32, 104; social imaginary of 8; temperament of 26–27; thought and 22–25; truth and 22

Pragmatism (Putnam) 11

problematic situations: doubt and 88–89; response to 94

progressive education: academic dimension of 120; activity-based 79–81; civic engagement in 121–122; collective power and 118; community and 124; creative dimension of 120; critiques of 8–9, 108; defining 124; democracy and 107; development of 4–5; Dewey and xi, 5, 10, 14; environmental issues in 122–123; global issues in 123–124; learning by doing in 79–80; Parker and xi; political dimension of 120–121; post-Civil War 17; public schools and 5; science and 4–5, 18; social change in 82, 109; social imaginary of 104; unequal power and 120; Young and xi

Progressive Education Association 109

public education: alienation in 78; compulsory education and 11, 71, 74, 91; conflict in 12; expose of 76–77; federal legislation and 11; progressive education and 5; reforms in 100; social change and 82–83

Putnam, Hilary 11, 14

Quine, W. V. 25

race: injustice and 110–111, 117–119; social class and 117, 119
racism 119
Rawls, John 62
reason 24, 45
responsibility: human agency and 32–33; in moral education 65–66
Rice, J. M. 76–78
Rorty, Richard 11, 14, 22
Russell, Bertrand 28–29

Sartre, Jean Paul xvii
Scheffler, Israel 108
School and Society (Dewey) 92
schooling: communal continuity and 73–75; defining 73; essential skills and 74; formal 73, 75, 99; reforms in 75–76, 91; segregated 109–110, 117, 122; socialization and 74–75
science: doubt and 32; liberating nature of 32; pragmatism and 8, 20–21, 30, 32, 104; progressive education and 4–5, 18; as a way of being 35; as a way of thinking 35
segregation 109–110, 117, 122
shared meanings 57–58
situated cognition 90
social behavior: character and 57; custom and 56–58; other-serving 58; social function of 66
social change: discussion and 117; education and 5, 19, 82–83, 117; new liberalism and xiii; oppressed groups and 82–83; tactics for 117–118
social class: education and 106; empowerment gap in 122; race and 117, 119; reproduction of unequal 8; Social Darwinism and 33
social cooperation 33–34
Social Darwinism 33–34
social imaginary: of American exceptionalism 111; assumptions of 6; changes in 116; competing 7; deconstructing 115–116; defining 5, 104; dimensions of 7; intelligibility in 7; of optimism and trust 7, 104–105, 108–109, 113; post-Civil War 26; pragmatism and 8; race in 118–119; of social progress 69, 108; of suspicion and distrust 109–112, 114, 116
socialization 74–75
social justice 62, 119
social science: liberating possibilities of 54–55; pragmatism and 21; social imaginary and 108

social systems 53
Spencer, Herbert 34
subject matter: child and 92; experience and 81; generation of interest and 108; method and 81, 83; pedagogy and 80–81; traditionalists and 73, 79, 92
Sumner, Charles 34

Taylor, Charles 5, 7, 104
teachers: in democratic education 95–96; as experts/novices 85, 87–88; historical methods and 85–86
thought: disruption of 23; engagement and 24; inquiry and 23; moral 59; moral knowledge and 63; pragmatism and 22–25; process of 22

Trotsky, Leon 15
truth: analytic 25; empiricist 22; James on 28–29; Peirce on 29; positivism and 25; pragmatism and 25; rationalist 22; warranted assertability (WA) and 23
"truthiness" 23

Waks, Leonard 10
warranted assertability (WA) 21–23, 28
Wartofsky, Marx xv, xvi, xix
West, Cornell 14, 116
West Virginia State Board of Education v. Barnette 11
wholeness 53–54
Wilson, Woodrow 106

Young, Ella Flagg xi